CONTENTS

· ·

SCANNING THE UNIVERSE

THE AGE OF
SPACE EXPLORATION

We haven't been exploring the cosmos for all that long. It was only in the 1940s that the first human-made object reached space. Since then, thousands of craft have blasted off from Earth, heading out into the cosmos on journeys of exploration. They've revealed many incredible wonders and even put men on the Moon. However, there is still so much more waiting to be discovered.

EXPLORING SPACE

Since ancient times, people have gazed into space and wondered what is out there. The invention of the telescope in the 17th century brought celestial objects into sharper focus (see p10). But we only began to see things first-hand once rockets powerful enough to reach space were created in the mid-20th century. In the decades since the first satellite was launched in 1957, unmanned spacecraft have travelled right across the Solar System, visiting planets and touching down on moons, asteroids and comets.

↓ SPACECRAFT HAVE EVEN LANDED WHEELED VEHICLES CALLED ROVERS, SUCH AS *CURIOSITY*, SHOWN HERE (SEE P60), ON THE SURFACE OF MARS.

SPACE TRAVEL

Perhaps the greatest achievement of the age of space exploration took place in 1969 when the first humans landed on the Moon as part of the *Apollo 11* mission (see p34). It marked a victory for the US in the Space Race, a rivalry between the then superpowers of the US and Soviet Union, which fuelled much early space exploration. However, in the early 1970s, the *Apollo* Moon missions ended and so did human exploration of other worlds – for now.

← THIS IMAGE SHOWS THE LAUNCH OF *APOLLO 11* ON 16 JULY 1969, TAKING THE FIRST HUMANS TO THE MOON.

OUR PLACE IN SPACE

As our understanding of the Universe has grown, so has our appreciation of just how small a part of it we are. There was a time when people thought Earth was the centre of (and made up most of) the Universe. We now know that space is unimaginably huge. Our Sun, which seems so vast to us, is just one of over 100 billion stars in our galaxy, the Milky Way. And there are over 100 billion galaxies. On this scale, Earth is just a tiny speck in the Universe.

TAKEN BY THE HUBBLE SPACE TELESCOPE (SEE P96), THIS IMAGE OF A TINY PATCH OF SKY CONTAINS THOUSANDS OF GALAXIES.

THE *VOYAGER* SPACECRAFT ARE OUT THERE SOMEWHERE TRAVELLING THE UNIVERSE.

SEEING MORE

Space is so vast that it takes a very long time to reach anywhere. Two spacecraft, *Voyager 1* and *Voyager 2*, have left our Solar System and are heading out into deep space (see p84). Despite travelling at thousands of kilometres an hour, it will take nearly 300,000 years for them to pass the next star. Without the invention of some as-yet-unknown form of transport, there is a limit to how far we can realistically travel. In the meanwhile, we can virtually explore the outer reaches of the Universe using powerful space telescopes such as Hubble (see p96).

LIVING IN SPACE

Between 1998 and 2011, a giant floating laboratory called the *International Space Station* was constructed in orbit high above Earth (see p46). Astronauts often live on the space station for months, conducting experiments. There has also been a recent revival of interest in space travel. Several private companies are planning to offer tourist trips high above Earth in the near future. And governments are renewing schemes to send humans into space. Plans for bases on the Moon, manned missions to Mars and even the colonisation of other worlds are all in the pipeline (see p106).

THIS ARTIST'S IMPRESSION OF HOW A MOON BASE COULD LOOK INCLUDES GREENHOUSES AND SOLAR PANELS.

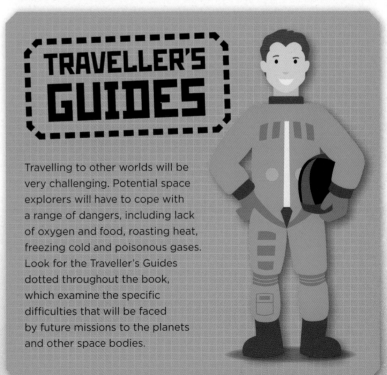

TRAVELLER'S GUIDES

Travelling to other worlds will be very challenging. Potential space explorers will have to cope with a range of dangers, including lack of oxygen and food, roasting heat, freezing cold and poisonous gases. Look for the Traveller's Guides dotted throughout the book, which examine the specific difficulties that will be faced by future missions to the planets and other space bodies.

SPACE EXPLORATION TIMELINE

For centuries, space exploration was little more than a fantasy. But in the mid-20th century, it finally became a reality with the creation of the first craft capable of reaching space. Since then, vast strides have been made and spacecraft have travelled further and further, first into Earth's orbit, then to the Moon and then out across the Solar System.

19 MAY 1961
Soviet craft *Venera 1* reaches Venus, becoming the first spacecraft to fly by another planet. However, radio contact is lost before it can send back any data.

16 MARCH 1926
'Father of Modern Rocketry' Robert Goddard launches the first liquid-fuelled rocket.

4 JANUARY 1959
The Soviet *Luna 1* becomes the first spacecraft to reach another world, the Moon. In September, its successor, *Luna 2*, deliberately crashes into the Moon's surface, becoming the first human-made object to make contact with another celestial body.

4 OCTOBER 1957
A Soviet Union *R-7* rocket launches *Sputnik 1*, the first satellite, into space.

20 JUNE 1944
Launched by Nazi Germany towards the end of the Second World War, a rocket-powered missile known as a *V-2* becomes the first human-made object to reach space.

3 NOVEMBER 1957
The first mammal in space, Laika the dog, is launched aboard Soviet *Sputnik 2*.

12 APRIL 1961
Soviet cosmonaut Yuri Gagarin becomes the first man in space aboard *Vostok 1*.

20 FEBRUARY 1947
Launched by the US in a captured *V-2* rocket, fruit flies become the first living creatures in space.

1975

1970

1965

1960

1955

1950

1945

1940

1935

1930

16 JUNE 1963
Soviet cosmonaut Valentina Tereshkova becomes the first woman in space aboard *Vostok 6*.

18 MARCH 1965
Soviet cosmonaut Alexei Leonov completes the first spacewalk from *Voskhod 2*.

20 JULY 1969
Apollo 11 lands human beings on the Moon for the first time.

19 APRIL 1971
The Soviets launch *Salyut 1*, the world's first space station. It's followed two years later by the US version, *Skylab*.

14 JULY 1965
After a flyby in 1962 by Soviet craft *Mars 1* failed to return pictures, the US probe *Mariner 4* makes the first successful flyby of Mars.

27 NOVEMBER 1971
Mars 2 crash-lands into Mars, becoming the first spacecraft to reach the planet's surface.

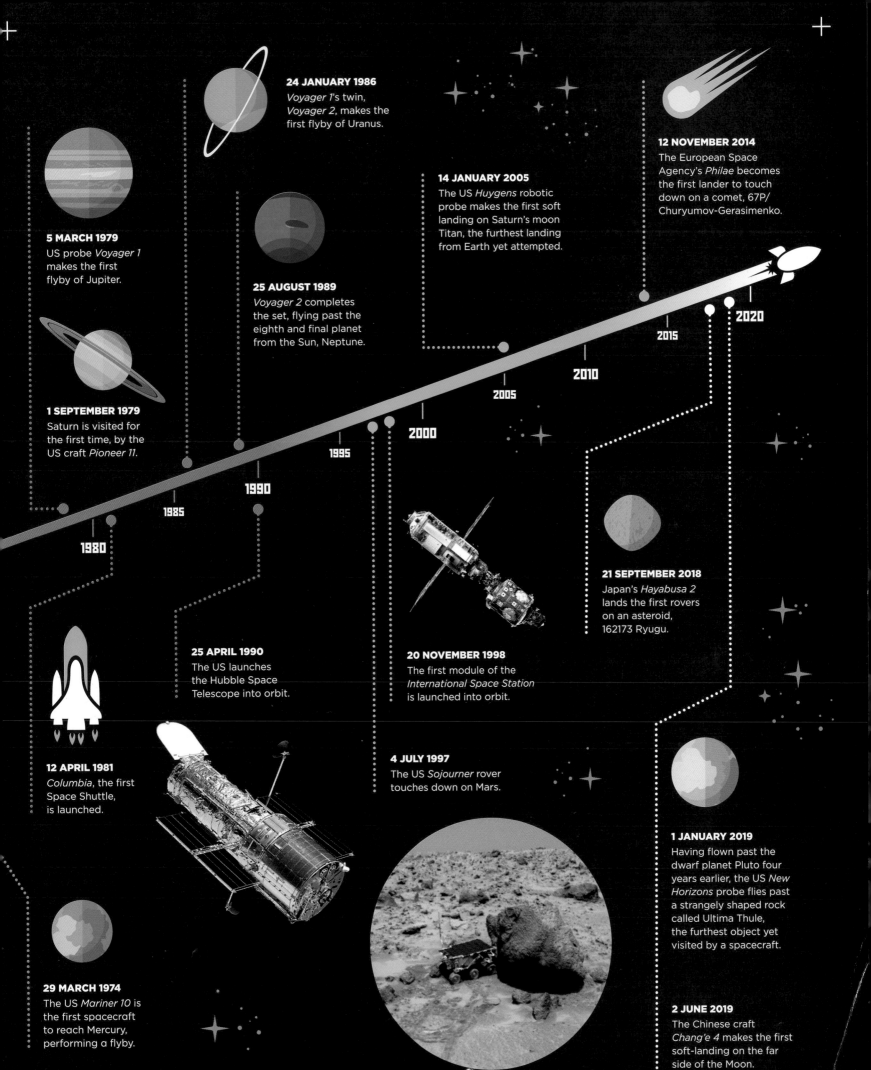

24 JANUARY 1986
Voyager 1's twin, Voyager 2, makes the first flyby of Uranus.

12 NOVEMBER 2014
The European Space Agency's Philae becomes the first lander to touch down on a comet, 67P/Churyumov-Gerasimenko.

14 JANUARY 2005
The US Huygens robotic probe makes the first soft landing on Saturn's moon Titan, the furthest landing from Earth yet attempted.

5 MARCH 1979
US probe Voyager 1 makes the first flyby of Jupiter.

25 AUGUST 1989
Voyager 2 completes the set, flying past the eighth and final planet from the Sun, Neptune.

1 SEPTEMBER 1979
Saturn is visited for the first time, by the US craft Pioneer 11.

2020

2015

2010

2005

2000

1995

1990

1985

1980

21 SEPTEMBER 2018
Japan's Hayabusa 2 lands the first rovers on an asteroid, 162173 Ryugu.

25 APRIL 1990
The US launches the Hubble Space Telescope into orbit.

20 NOVEMBER 1998
The first module of the International Space Station is launched into orbit.

12 APRIL 1981
Columbia, the first Space Shuttle, is launched.

4 JULY 1997
The US Sojourner rover touches down on Mars.

1 JANUARY 2019
Having flown past the dwarf planet Pluto four years earlier, the US New Horizons probe flies past a strangely shaped rock called Ultima Thule, the furthest object yet visited by a spacecraft.

29 MARCH 1974
The US Mariner 10 is the first spacecraft to reach Mercury, performing a flyby.

2 JUNE 2019
The Chinese craft Chang'e 4 makes the first soft-landing on the far side of the Moon.

THE FIRST ASTRONOMERS

Ancient civilisations believed the stars made divine patterns in the sky. Early astronomers looked for reasons that explained the movements of the Sun, Moon and planets. Astronomy, the study of the stars, planets and space, is often regarded as the world's oldest science.

THE TIME-MEASURING SKY

Early astronomers used the movements of the Sun, Moon and stars to measure time. A day was measured by one sunrise to the next. A lunar month (29.53 days) was measured from one full Moon to the next. Stars move across the sky every night, but also change with the seasons. The appearance of the star Sirius in spring told ancient Egyptian farmers that the Nile was about to flood. The life-giving waters of the Nile nourished the dry, desert soil, making it fertile for the farmer's crops.

⊘ THIS SHOWS HOW THE MOON APPEARS IN THE NIGHT SKY OVER THE COURSE OF A MONTH.

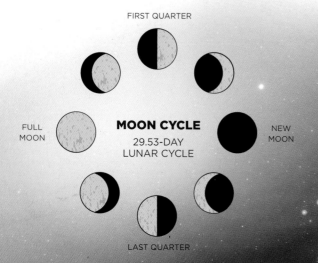

FIRST QUARTER

MOON CYCLE
29.53-DAY
LUNAR CYCLE

FULL MOON

NEW MOON

LAST QUARTER

CONSTELLATION OF ORION.

SIRIUS, ALSO KNOWN AS THE DOG STAR, SEEN ABOVE EGYPT. IT IS THE BRIGHTEST STAR IN THE SKY AND PART OF THE CONSTELLATION CANIS MINOR.

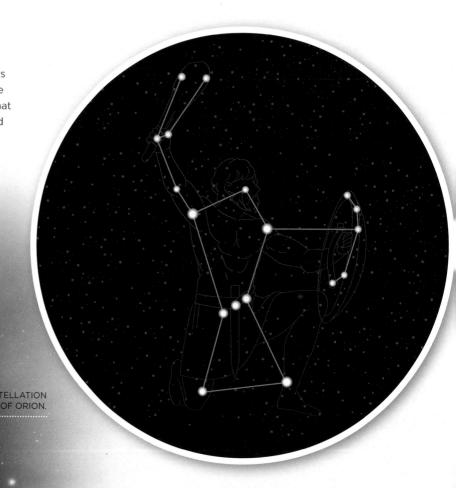

⊕ ORION IS VISIBLE FROM BOTH THE SOUTHERN AND NORTHERN HEMISPHERES AT DIFFERENT TIMES OF THE YEAR.

CIVILISATIONS AND CONSTELLATIONS

Ancient people were more familiar with the night sky than we are today. Some believed the Sun, Moon and stars to be gods. Others imagined patterns of stars created pictures, which they named after creatures and heroes of myth and legend. We still use many of these names today. We call these star patterns constellations. A famous constellation is Orion, named by ancient Greek astronomers after a mythical hunter.

PTOLEMY'S PLANETS

Ptolemy (c100ce–c170ce) was an ancient Egyptian astronomer of Greek descent who described Earth as a large, round ball. Before the Greeks, many people thought Earth was flat. In 150ce, Ptolemy wrote that Earth was positioned at the centre of a series of hollow spheres. The Sun and the planets were each fixed to the inside of one of these spheres, which all rotated round Earth. Although Ptolemy's theory was incorrect, people believed it for nearly 1400 years.

A 17TH-CENTURY REPRESENTATION OF PTOLEMY'S GEOCENTRIC MODEL OF THE UNIVERSE, WITH EARTH AT THE CENTRE.

A 15TH-CENTURY IMAGE OF PTOLEMY.

CORRECTED BY COPERNICUS

In 1543, a Polish monk called Copernicus wrote that the five then-known planets – Mercury, Venus, Mars, Jupiter and Saturn – were actually in orbit around the Sun. Later that century, Danish astronomer Tycho Brahe and his assistant Johannes Kepler confirmed Copernicus' theory. Kepler worked out that the planets did not move in perfect circles around the Sun, but in oval paths called ellipses.

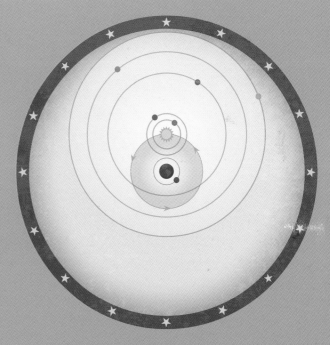

THE TYCHONIC SYSTEM FROM THE 16TH CENTURY COMBINED THE COPERNICAN AND PTOLEMAIC SYSTEMS, WITH THE SUN ROTATING ROUND EARTH BUT THE OTHER PLANETS ROTATING ROUND THE SUN.

BRAHE AND KEPLER'S DANISH OBSERVATORY, SHOWN HERE, WAS PACKED FULL OF INSTRUMENTS FOR TRACKING THE MOVEMENT OF THE PLANETS.

GEOCENTRIC MODEL

According to this theory, Earth is at the centre, and the Sun orbits the planet.

HELIOCENTRIC MODEL

Later, scientists revealed that Earth – and the other planets – orbit the Sun.

EARTH TELESCOPES

The first astronomers were equipped with only the naked eye so they could not see far into space. This changed with the 1608 invention of the telescope, which uses curved pieces of glass called lenses to make distant objects seem larger and nearer. It changed human understanding of the Universe and our place within it for ever.

GROUND-BREAKING GALILEO

In 1609, an Italian scientist named Galileo Galilei developed a refracting telescope (see opposite) that could magnify objects by up to 20 times. Galileo used it to show that the Moon was not smooth, but pockmarked by craters, and discovered four moons circling Jupiter, which confirmed Copernicus' theory that some celestial bodies did not orbit Earth. The then hugely powerful Catholic Church in Italy did not accept Galileo's findings. The Church incorrectly believed that Earth was at the centre of the Universe.

PAINTING SHOWING GALILEO DEMONSTRATING HIS TELESCOPE IN VENICE. HE WAS LATER IMPRISONED BY THE CHURCH AND SPENT THE REST OF HIS LIFE UNDER HOUSE ARREST.

GALILEO DREW LUNAR CRATERS AND OTHER FEATURES BASED ON WHAT HE COULD SEE THROUGH HIS TELESCOPE.

A REPLICA OF THE REFLECTING TELESCOPE THAT NEWTON DESIGNED AND BUILT.

REFLECTING ON NEWTON

In around 1687, an English scientist named Isaac Newton developed a new telescope called a reflecting telescope, or reflector, that used mirrors instead of lenses. This made distant objects look clearer than earlier refracting telescopes. Newton is famous for discovering gravity, which is the force that pulls things towards each other. Gravity pulls us down to the surface of Earth, holds the Moon in orbit around Earth, and keeps Earth and the planets in our Solar System in orbit around the Sun.

10.4m
(31.4ft)

DIAMETER OF THE GRAN
TELESCOPIO CANARIAS
MIRROR

THE LARGEST TELESCOPE IN THE WORLD IS THE GRAN TELESCOPIO
CANARIAS (ABOVE). HOWEVER, A NEW EXTREMELY LARGE TELESCOPE
(ELT) IS BEING BUILT WITH A MAMMOTH 39.3m (130ft) MIRROR.

HERSCHEL GOES HUGE

In the late 18th century, English astronomer William Herschel
built large, reflecting telescopes to see further into space
than ever before. In 1781, he used one to discover a new
planet, Uranus (see p78). His largest telescope, built a few
years later, contained a mirror 122cm (48in) in diameter, which
was considered enormous at the time. Today massive telescopes
built at high-up observatories are grouped together to explore
the sky. At high altitudes telescopes suffer less interference
from city lights or the atmosphere.

RADIO UNIVERSE

Radio telescopes have large dishes and antennae to detect
radio-frequency radiation given out by objects in space.

RADIO TELESCOPES AT THE VERY LARGE ARRAY, THE
NATIONAL RADIO OBSERVATORY IN NEW MEXICO.

REFRACTING vs REFLECTING TELESCOPES

There are two types of optical telescope,
which create images by gathering visible light.

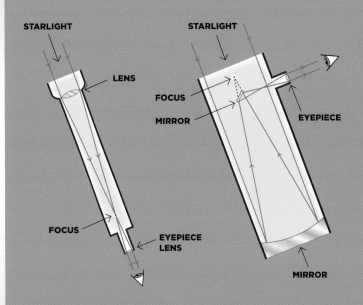

STARLIGHT

LENS

FOCUS

FOCUS

EYEPIECE
LENS

STARLIGHT

FOCUS

MIRROR

EYEPIECE

MIRROR

REFRACTING TELESCOPES
gather and focus light through
a large, front lens. This creates
an image that can be viewed
through an eyepiece.

REFLECTING TELESCOPES use
a large mirror to collect visible
light and then reflect the image
to the viewer's eyepiece or
camera via a smaller mirror.

THE FIRST ROCKETS

The main obstacle facing anything trying to get into space is gravity. To overcome the pull of gravity and get an object into orbit, a huge upward thrust must take place. Only a rocket has the power to do this. However, the first rockets were not designed to explore space. Instead, they were developed as weapons of war.

FIREWORKS TO WARHEADS

An explosive substance known as a propellant is required to launch a rocket upwards. The first propellant was gunpowder, invented by the Chinese in the 10th century for use in fireworks. In 1805, British officer William Congreve built a gunpowder-propelled rocket that carried a cargo, or payload, of gunpowder in its nose (see below). Designed to fly around 2km (1 mile) and explode on impact, this was the first warhead missile.

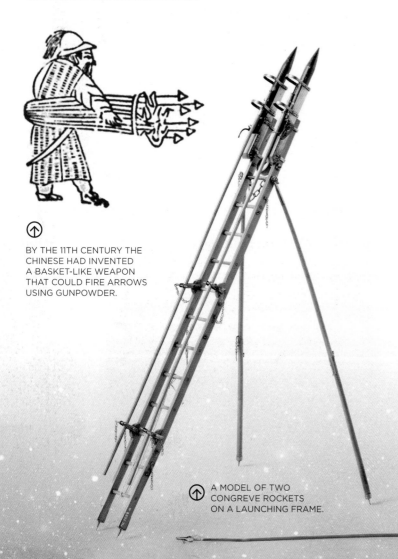

⊕ BY THE 11TH CENTURY THE CHINESE HAD INVENTED A BASKET-LIKE WEAPON THAT COULD FIRE ARROWS USING GUNPOWDER.

⊕ A MODEL OF TWO CONGREVE ROCKETS ON A LAUNCHING FRAME.

⊕ KONSTANTIN TSIOLKOVSKY STANDING IN HIS STUDIO WITH TWO METAL AIRSHIP MODELS.

TSIOLKOVSKY'S THEORIES

Konstantin Tsiolkovsky (1857–1935) was a Russian scientist who became obsessed with the possibility of firing a rocket into space. To achieve orbit, Tsiolkovsky calculated that a rocket needs to obtain a speed of 7.9km/sec (4.9 miles/sec), or 28,000km/h (18,000mph). This is known as orbital velocity. A rocket would need a far stronger propellant than gunpowder to achieve this. Tsiolkovsky suggested a liquid propellant of hydrogen and oxygen, with extra fuel carried on board the rocket itself to be used in a series of stages.

GODDARD ADVANCES

In 1926, American professor Robert Goddard proved Tsiolkovsky's theories correct by launching the first liquid-fuelled rocket. Powered by gasoline and liquid oxygen, Goddard's *Nell* flew for two-and-a-half seconds and reached an altitude of 12m (39ft). Goddard went on to develop rockets that could fly faster than the speed of sound and, like Tsiolkovsky, proposed a rocket that would use stages to take people into space.

⟵ TODAY KNOWN AS THE FATHER OF MODERN ROCKETRY, HERE GODDARD STANDS NEXT TO THE WORLD'S FIRST LIQUID-FUELLED ROCKET, CALLED *NELL*.

THE VENGEANCE ROCKET

During the 1920s and 1930s, amateur rocket societies sprang up across Europe. Germany's Verein für Raumschiffahrt ('Society for Space Travel') made advances, spurred on by the work of engineers Hermann Oberth and Wernher von Braun. In the mid 1930s, von Braun became technical director of the Nazi Party's rocket programme. Using Goddard's theory of liquid-fuelled rockets, von Braun developed the *Vengeance Weapon 2*, or *V-2*. A flying bomb, it could fly for 320km (200 miles) in six minutes. Over 3000 *V-2* rockets hit London and Antwerp during the Second World War.

⟶ THE NAZI *V-2* WAS YEARS AHEAD OF THE REST OF THE WORLD. THE ALLIES BECAME DESPERATE TO LAY THEIR HANDS ON THE *V-2* ROCKET TECHNOLOGY.

HOW ROCKETS WORK

A rocket uses the principle of action and reaction to move. This happens when exploding gas escapes from a rocket's nozzle in one direction and the rocket is propelled in the other.

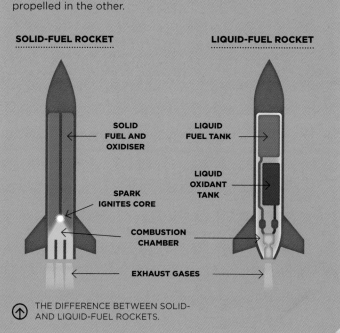

SOLID-FUEL ROCKET

LIQUID-FUEL ROCKET

SOLID FUEL AND OXIDISER

LIQUID FUEL TANK

LIQUID OXIDANT TANK

SPARK IGNITES CORE

COMBUSTION CHAMBER

EXHAUST GASES

⬆ THE DIFFERENCE BETWEEN SOLID- AND LIQUID-FUEL ROCKETS.

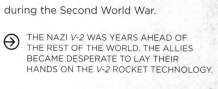

THE SPACE RACE

Following the Second World War, two superpowers emerged: the United States and the Soviet Union. Both raced to get hold of secret German rocket technology. This began an intense competition between the two rivals, known as the Space Race.

ROCKETS FROM THE ASHES

Invading soldiers from both the United States (US) and Soviet Union (USSR) searched Germany for unused *V-2*s. A missile that could travel for over 300km (200 miles) across international borders was much desired. Hundreds of *V-2* rockets were discovered at a secret factory beneath a hill in east-central Germany. Some of the *V-2* scientists were captured by Soviet soldiers, but the greatest prize fell to the Americans, when *V-2* designer Wernher von Braun surrendered to US troops.

⬆ GERMAN ROCKET SCIENTISTS, INCLUDING VON BRAUN, SHOWN IN THE CENTRE WITH A BROKEN ARM, PICTURED AFTER THEIR SURRENDER IN 1945.

WERNHER VON BRAUN

Although Wernher von Braun had been a lieutenant in the Nazi SS, his rocket expertise was considered of vital importance to the US. He was therefore allowed to settle in America in return for becoming technical director of the country's ballistic-weapons programme. In the 1950s, von Braun became an instrumental part of America's space programme and was made a director of the newly formed National Aeronautics and Space Administration (NASA). He led the design of the *Saturn V* rocket that would send men to the Moon in the 1960s.

⬆ US POLITICIANS INSPECTING A *V-2* FACTORY SHORTLY BEFORE THE END OF THE SECOND WORLD WAR. AN ESTIMATED 25,000 SLAVE LABOURERS DIED THERE CONSTRUCTING *V-2* ROCKETS.

DESPITE INSISTING THAT HE HAD BEEN FORCED TO BE PART OF THE NAZI WAR MACHINE, VON BRAUN WAS NEVER ALLOWED TO COMPLETELY FORGET HIS CONTROVERSIAL PAST. HERE HE IS PHOTOGRAPHED IN 1960 AS DIRECTOR OF NASA'S MARSHALL SPACE FLIGHT CENTER.

THE COLD WAR

The decades-long rivalry between the US and the USSR after the Second World War was called the Cold War. The two sides did not come into direct conflict, but the threat of nuclear war lay in the background. The Space Race was one way this rivalry played out. There was a great fear of what could be achieved on a military front by a nation that built rockets that were capable of reaching space.

THIS SOVIET PROPAGANDA POSTER FEATURES A FEMALE COSMONAUT AND THE CAPTION 'CONQUERING THE COSMOS!'

KOROLEV, FAR RIGHT, SHOWN HERE WITH YURI GAGARIN, SECOND FROM LEFT (SEE P22), WAS ABLE TO EXPAND ON THE *V-2* DESIGN TO BUILD THE *R-7*, THE MOST POWERFUL ROCKET THE WORLD HAD SEEN.

SERGEI KOROLEV

Soviet rocket scientist Sergei Korolev was Wernher von Braun's opposite number in the Space Race. Korolev was made chief designer of spacecraft after spending six years in a Soviet Gulag, or prison camp. But the world knew little of his achievements as he was never referred to by name in official announcements by the Soviet government, so as to maintain strict secrecy. Korolev's genius, however, easily matched that of his rival von Braun. The scientist would personally keep the Soviets in the lead for the important first years of the Space Race.

FIRST IN ORBIT

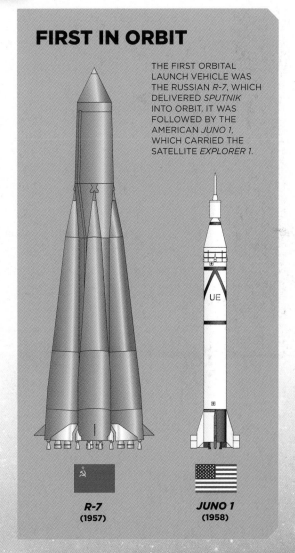

THE FIRST ORBITAL LAUNCH VEHICLE WAS THE RUSSIAN *R-7*, WHICH DELIVERED *SPUTNIK* INTO ORBIT. IT WAS FOLLOWED BY THE AMERICAN *JUNO 1*, WHICH CARRIED THE SATELLITE *EXPLORER 1*.

R-7
(1957)

JUNO 1
(1958)

SPUTNIK

In 1957, the Soviet Union stunned the world by launching the first satellite into space – a satellite is an object that orbits a planet or star. *Sputnik 1* was a beachball-sized device launched atop the most powerful rocket yet created, the mighty *R-7*. This achievement put the Soviets ahead in the Space Race and was a bitter blow to their US rivals.

↑ AFTER THREE WEEKS AND 1400 ORBITS, *SPUTNIK*'S BATTERIES RAN FLAT. TWO MONTHS LATER IT BURNED UP IN EARTH'S ATMOSPHERE.

SPUTNIK 1

Launched on 4 October 1957, *Sputnik 1* was a metal ball with four antennae that sent out radio beeps as it orbited Earth. The beeps could be picked up by radio receivers around the world, but, like the satellite itself, they served no practical function. *Sputnik* was instead simply a symbol of Soviet propaganda. It showed the Soviet Union now had a rocket that could reach Earth's orbit and also travel over American soil.

FLOPNIK

After *Sputnik*, the US raced to send its own satellite into orbit. The launch of *Vanguard TV-3* (6 December 1957) was marked by much fanfare, but failed to live up to expectations. The rocket carrying the satellite rose only 1m (3ft) into the air before crashing back to Earth and toppling over. The satellite rolled out from the top of the rocket and continued sending radio beeps. The launch had been a humiliating disaster.

← THE LAUNCH OF *VANGUARD TV-3* RECEIVED DAMNING HEADLINES IN US NEWSPAPERS THAT PLAYED ON THE WORD *SPUTNIK*, SUCH AS 'FLOPNIK' AND 'KAPUTNIK'.

'...they have put one small ball in the air.'

President Eisenhower tries to downplay the Soviet achievement.

EXPLORER 1
AMERICA'S FIRST EARTH SATELLITE

jpl
JET PROPULSION LABORATORY
CALIFORNIA INSTITUTE OF TECHNOLOGY

EXPLORER 1

The *Vanguard TV-3* satellite had been the brainchild of the US Navy. Now, after the Navy's embarrassing failure, the government turned to Wernher von Braun, who promised to launch a new satellite into space within 90 days. *Explorer 1* was a javelin-shaped satellite that sat atop a *Juno 1* rocket. On 31 January 1958, *Explorer 1* was launched without a hitch. The US was back in the Space Race.

THIS IMAGE WAS CREATED BY NASA'S JET PROPULSION LABORATORY TO CELEBRATE THE CIGAR-SHAPED SATELLITE'S SUCCESSFUL LAUNCH.

REACHING ORBIT

Spacecraft going into orbit around Earth need to maintain a certain speed to avoid being dragged down to Earth. This varies according to altitude, but at 240km (150 miles) above Earth, a spacecraft needs to be travelling at 7.6km/sec (4.7 miles/sec). To break free of a planet's gravity, a rocket must reach a speed known as the escape velocity. A spacecraft leaving Earth needs to travel at an escape velocity of at least 11.2km/sec (6.96 miles/sec).

ESCAPE VELOCITY
IF A SPACECRAFT CONTINUES AT ESCAPE VELOCITY, IT WILL SOON LEAVE EARTH FAR BEHIND.

ORBITAL VELOCITY
IF A SPACECRAFT MAINTAINS ITS SPEED IN ORBIT, IT WILL STAY THERE FOREVER.

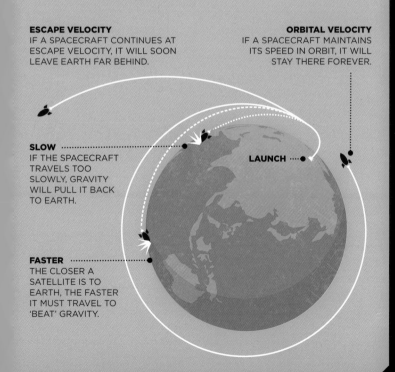

SLOW
IF THE SPACECRAFT TRAVELS TOO SLOWLY, GRAVITY WILL PULL IT BACK TO EARTH.

LAUNCH

FASTER
THE CLOSER A SATELLITE IS TO EARTH, THE FASTER IT MUST TRAVEL TO 'BEAT' GRAVITY.

VANGUARD 1

In March 1958, the US Navy was once again allowed to try to launch a satellite, *Vanguard 1*. It was programmed to record data about Earth's outer atmosphere. However, unlike *Explorer 1*, *Vanguard 1* was powered by solar cells rather than batteries. This meant it was able to continue transmitting data back to Earth until 1965. It remains in orbit to this day.

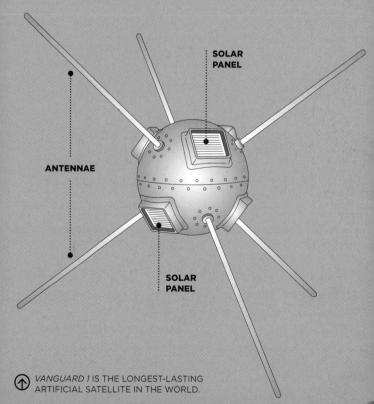

SOLAR PANEL

ANTENNAE

SOLAR PANEL

VANGUARD 1 IS THE LONGEST-LASTING ARTIFICIAL SATELLITE IN THE WORLD.

SATELLITES

The Moon is a natural satellite that orbits Earth, but all of our other satellites are artificial. Since the 1957 launch of the first artificial satellite, *Sputnik 1*, around 9000 satellites have been blasted into orbit. These satellites help people on Earth communicate, navigate and observe the environment.

DIFFERENT ORBITS

Satellites can orbit Earth at different distances. The closer a satellite is to Earth, the faster it will complete its orbit.

A LOW-EARTH ORBIT
160km (100 miles)

A MEDIUM-EARTH ORBIT
20,350km (12,645 miles)

A HIGH-EARTH ORBIT
35,800km (22,200 miles), but some satellites orbit even higher

COMMUNICATIONS SATELLITES

Communications satellites give people on Earth 24-hour access to information and each other. Satellites do this by picking up television, radio, telephone and internet signals from one place and beaming them back to different places on Earth.

THE SPACE SHUTTLE (SEE P44) DEPLOYING A COMMUNICATIONS SATELLITE ON 27 AUGUST 1985.

NAVIGATION SATELLITES

Several satellites working together, such as the ones that make up the US-operated Global Positioning System (GPS), can help people on Earth navigate by sending signals to a receiver, such as a smartphone. By calculating the time it takes for signals from at least four satellites to reach it, the receiver can work out its distance from each one and, from that, its exact location on Earth.

WHEN THIS SATELLITE IS NO LONGER NEEDED, IT MAY BE SENT INTO A 'GRAVEYARD ORBIT' HIGH ABOVE EARTH OUT OF THE REACH OF OTHER SATELLITES.

SPY SATELLITES

Reconnaissance satellites are used by governments and the military to spy on other countries. They are top secret, so the exact number of them in orbit around Earth is unknown.

WEATHER AND ENVIRONMENTAL SATELLITES

Weather and environmental satellites monitor conditions on Earth's surface and report the information to stations on the ground. Weather satellite data includes everything from cloud cover and air temperature to wind speed and wave height. Environmental satellites provide a view of changes, such as shrinking ice fields and reductions of lakes and rivers.

GOES-16 IS A WEATHER SATELLITE IN GEOSTATIONARY ORBIT, ORBITING AT THE SAME SPEED AS EARTH, WHICH KEEPS IT STATIONARY IN THE SKY ALWAYS OVER THE SAME POINT.

SPACE JUNK

It is estimated that of the roughly 9000 artificial satellites launched since 1957, around 5000 are still in orbit. Many have fallen back to Earth or burned up during re-entry. Others have broken up and become part of the vast mass of debris known as space junk. There are estimated to be over 8400 tonnes (8000 tons) of space junk in Earth's orbit, ranging from flecks of paint to dead satellites.

20,000

MORE THAN 20,000 OBJECTS LARGER THAN A SOFTBALL ARE IN EARTH'S ORBIT

SATELLITE DESTRUCTION

In 2007, China used a ballistic missile to destroy one of its weather satellites. This resulted in a cloud of debris in Earth's orbit.

SATELLITE COLLISION

Even more debris was generated in 2009 when two communications satellites accidentally collided. The American *Iridium 33* and Russian *Cosmos 2251* had both been in orbit since the 1990s.

28,000km/h

(17,400mph)

Space junk poses a serious risk to future space missions. Objects in orbit around Earth travel at around 28,000km/h (17,400mph). At this speed, even a fleck of paint can crack a spacecraft window.

SPACE CREATURES

With the first spacecraft launched into orbit, the race was on to put human travellers up there. Launching just a month after _Sputnik 1_, _Sputnik 2_ carried on board a passenger – Laika the dog. Laika – along with several other animals over the next few years – would pave the way for human missions.

SENDING A STRAY

Laika was a stray dog picked for the _Sputnik 2_ mission because of her calm nature. She was willing to sit for hours in a tightly confined space, dressed in a dog nappy to collect her waste. Laika survived the launch of _Sputnik 2_ on 3 November 1957, but after 103 minutes the spacecraft's heat shield malfunctioned and the temperature on board rocketed. Laika probably died from a combination of heat and stress.

LAIKA WAS THE FIRST ANIMAL TO GO INTO ORBIT AROUND EARTH.

A REPLICA OF _SPUTNIK 2_, THE SPACECRAFT LAIKA TRAVELLED IN.

EARLY ANIMALS

Laika received a great deal of attention around the globe, but the Soviet Union and United States had already launched several animals aboard rockets. In 1947, the US sent fruit flies on a suborbital flight. This meant they reached space by crossing the boundary known as the Kármán line 100km (62 miles) above sea level, but did not complete an orbit. The flies returned unharmed. In 1948, a rhesus monkey called Albert was launched aboard a _V-2 Blossom_ rocket but did not survive the flight. It took until 1959 for two female monkeys – Miss Able and Miss Baker – to return safely. Miss Baker lived for another 25 years.

BELKA (LEFT) AND STRELKA (RIGHT) WERE THE FIRST DOGS TO SURVIVE ORBITING EARTH.

BELKA AND STRELKA

In 1960, the dogs Belka and Strelka were successfully launched into space along with a rabbit, two rats and 42 mice. Soon after reaching Earth's orbit, there was no movement from either dog. Then after four orbits, Belka vomited and both dogs started barking. They were alive! Belka and Strelka returned safely to Earth as global celebrities, after one day in space. The rabbit, rats and mice also survived.

IN 1959 MISS BAKER, A SQUIRREL MONKEY, BECAME THE FIRST MAMMAL TO SURVIVE A TRIP TO SPACE.

AFTER HUMANS

The role of animals in space changed following the Moon landing in 1969. After that, animals were sent into space on missions to test out the long-term effects of weightlessness or whether it was possible to mate in space. Two spiders were sent on a mission aboard the space station *Skylab* in 1973. The spiders, called Anita and Arabella, were recorded trying to spin webs in space. They both struggled with the task initially, but after adapting to the microgravity conditions, the spiders learned to weave a perfect web once more.

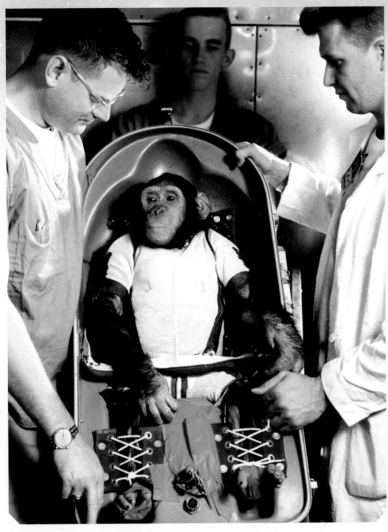

CHIMPANZEE HAM PREPARING FOR HIS SPACE FLIGHT ON 31 JANUARY 1961.

HELPING HAM

In 1961, the US staged a final dress rehearsal for its first human flight. It launched Ham the chimpanzee on a suborbital flight for 15 minutes. During the flight, Ham experienced over six minutes of near weightlessness. Despite onboard cameras recording some distress during take off and landing, Ham was able to perform the tasks he had been trained for before the flight and the mission was a success. Ham returned safely and lived until 1983.

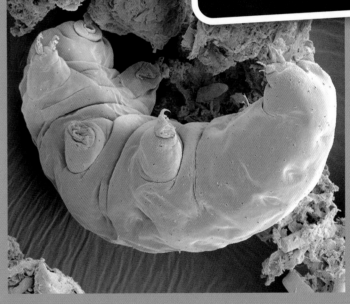

IN 2019, THOUSANDS OF TARDIGRADES – MICROSCOPIC CREATURES ALSO KNOWN AS WATER BEARS – ARRIVED ON THE MOON WHEN A LUNAR LANDER CRASHED. TARDIGRADES CAN WITHSTAND EXTREME CONDITIONS, SO IT'S POSSIBLE SOME MAY HAVE SURVIVED.

SPACE ANIMALS IN NUMBERS

108km
(68 miles)

Altitude reached in 1947 by the first animals – fruit flies – to visit outer space.

32

Total number of monkeys to have flown in space.

22

Number of days that Russian dogs Vetrok and Ugolyok orbited Earth for in 1966. This is still the longest canine space flight.

2000+

Number of creatures sent into space on the shuttle *Columbia* on 17 April 1998.

THE FIRST ASTRONAUT

In 1961, the Soviet Union achieved its greatest Space Race first. On 12 April, it blasted cosmonaut Yuri Gagarin into Earth's orbit on board *Vostok 1*. This made Gagarin the first human to be launched into space and made the Soviet Union the leading nation in the Space Race – for now.

6.12am
THE CORE ROCKET STAGE FINISHES ITS FUEL AND FALLS AWAY AS THE FINAL ROCKET STAGE FIRES UP.

YURI GAGARIN PREPARING FOR TAKE OFF ON *VOSTOK 1*.

R-7 ROCKET

The world's first intercontinental ballistic missile, the *R-7* rocket had previously launched the *Sputnik* satellites before being used for the *Vostok* missions.

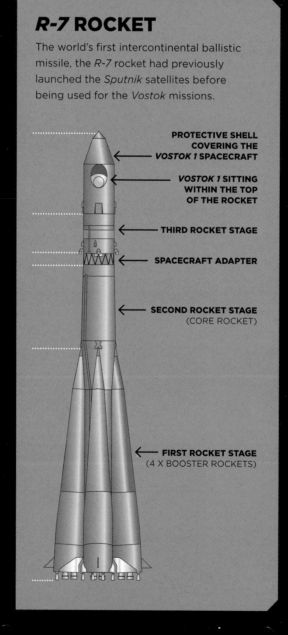

PROTECTIVE SHELL COVERING THE *VOSTOK 1* SPACECRAFT

VOSTOK 1 SITTING WITHIN THE TOP OF THE ROCKET

THIRD ROCKET STAGE

SPACECRAFT ADAPTER

SECOND ROCKET STAGE (CORE ROCKET)

FIRST ROCKET STAGE (4 X BOOSTER ROCKETS)

6.10am
THE SHELL COVERING *VOSTOK 1* AT THE FRONT OF THE *R-7* ROCKET FALLS AWAY. GAGARIN CAN NOW SEE EARTH BELOW HIM.

6.09am
THE *R-7*'S FOUR BOOSTER ROCKETS BURN THROUGH THEIR FUEL AND FALL AWAY.

VOSTOK PLAN

Vostok 1 was a small capsule launched atop a three-stage *R-7* rocket designed to take Yuri Gagarin into space. After one orbit around Earth, *Vostok 1* would parachute down 108 minutes later.

VOSTOK SPACECRAFT

Vostok 1 was made up of two parts: a descent module and an instrument module. The descent module contained Gagarin's ejector seat, control panel and the retro rockets that would slow *Vostok 1* down for re-entry. Although *Vostok 1* had a control panel, the spacecraft was fully automated.

BLAST-OFF
AT 6.07am (MOSCOW TIME), *VOSTOK 1* BLASTS OFF FROM THE BAIKONUR COSMODROME AS YURI GAGARIN SHOUTS *'POYEKHALI!'* ('LET'S ROLL!').

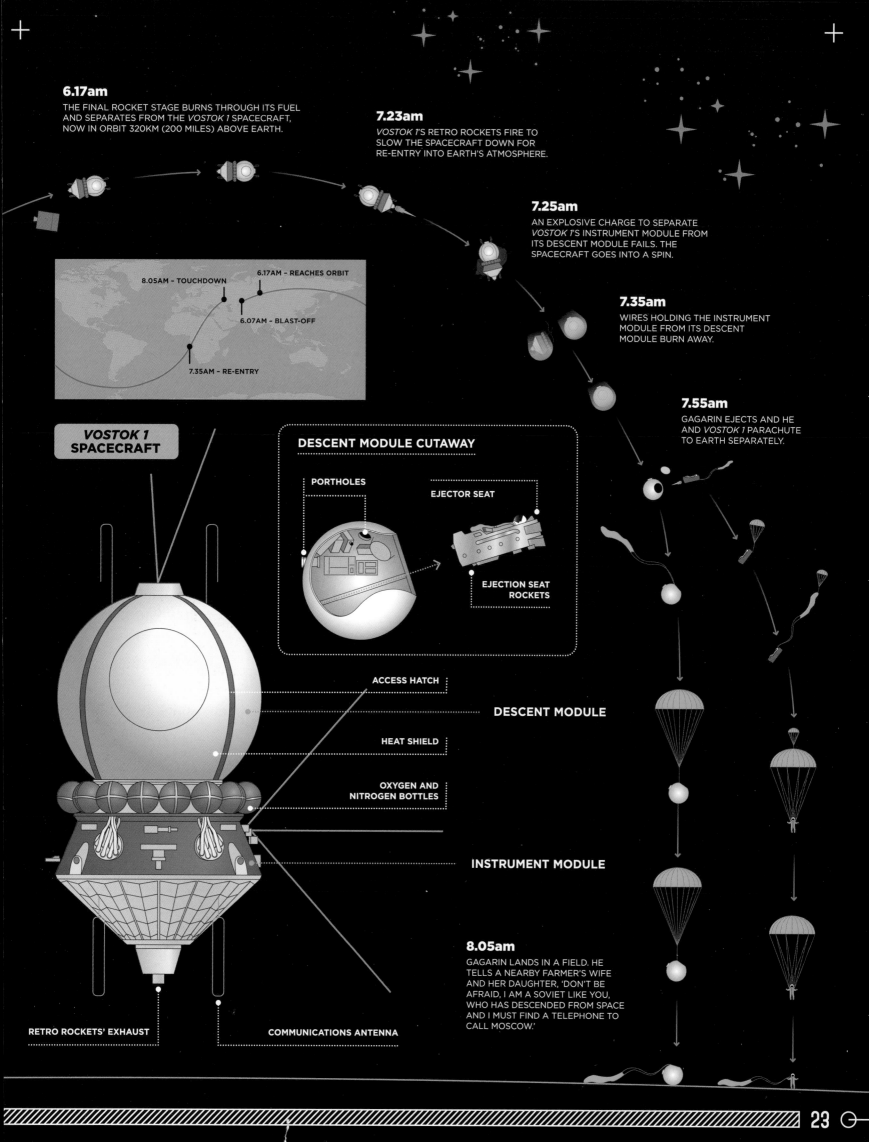

6.17am
THE FINAL ROCKET STAGE BURNS THROUGH ITS FUEL AND SEPARATES FROM THE *VOSTOK 1* SPACECRAFT, NOW IN ORBIT 320KM (200 MILES) ABOVE EARTH.

7.23am
VOSTOK 1'S RETRO ROCKETS FIRE TO SLOW THE SPACECRAFT DOWN FOR RE-ENTRY INTO EARTH'S ATMOSPHERE.

7.25am
AN EXPLOSIVE CHARGE TO SEPARATE *VOSTOK 1*'S INSTRUMENT MODULE FROM ITS DESCENT MODULE FAILS. THE SPACECRAFT GOES INTO A SPIN.

7.35am
WIRES HOLDING THE INSTRUMENT MODULE FROM ITS DESCENT MODULE BURN AWAY.

7.55am
GAGARIN EJECTS AND HE AND *VOSTOK 1* PARACHUTE TO EARTH SEPARATELY.

8.05AM – TOUCHDOWN   6.17AM – REACHES ORBIT

6.07AM – BLAST-OFF

7.35AM – RE-ENTRY

VOSTOK 1 SPACECRAFT

DESCENT MODULE CUTAWAY

PORTHOLES

EJECTOR SEAT

EJECTION SEAT ROCKETS

ACCESS HATCH

DESCENT MODULE

HEAT SHIELD

OXYGEN AND NITROGEN BOTTLES

INSTRUMENT MODULE

8.05am
GAGARIN LANDS IN A FIELD. HE TELLS A NEARBY FARMER'S WIFE AND HER DAUGHTER, 'DON'T BE AFRAID, I AM A SOVIET LIKE YOU, WHO HAS DESCENDED FROM SPACE AND I MUST FIND A TELEPHONE TO CALL MOSCOW.'

RETRO ROCKETS' EXHAUST   COMMUNICATIONS ANTENNA

SPACE PIONEERS

After Yuri Gagarin became the first man in orbit, the United States was desperate to catch up. In the early 1960s, the US announced a series of increasingly ambitious manned space missions. The Soviet Union, however, continued to set the pace. That was until an announcement upped the stakes for both sides.

SHEPARD STARTS

Under increasing pressure to send its own astronaut into space, NASA finally delivered on 2 May 1961. Alan Shepard blasted off aboard *Freedom 7*, one of a series of *Mercury* spacecraft that were smaller and lighter than the Soviet *Vostoks*. But unlike *Vostok*, the *Mercury* spacecraft were fitted with a joystick so the astronaut could take control. However, the *Mercury-Redstone* rocket carrying the *Freedom 7* spacecraft was only powerful enough to take it on a suborbital flight.

→ ALAN SHEPARD IN HIS *MERCURY* FLIGHT SUIT. HE SPENT 15 MINUTES IN SPACE ABOARD *FREEDOM 7* BEFORE SPLASHING DOWN INTO THE ATLANTIC OCEAN.

⬆ THE USSR'S SECOND COSMONAUT, GHERMAN TITOV (PICTURED HERE IN HIS FLIGHT SUIT) ORBITED EARTH 17.5 TIMES IN A RECORD-BREAKING VOYAGE THAT LASTED 25 HOURS AND 18 MINUTES.

TITOV TAKES TITLES

Determined to retain its Space Race lead, the Soviet Union launched its most daring mission yet. On 6 August 1961, cosmonaut Gherman Titov was launched into orbit aboard *Vostok 2*. His mission was to be the first person to spend a whole day in space and film Earth from his spacecraft. He also achieved the more dubious honour of being the first human to vomit in space. His successful mission, however, put the Soviets out in front once more.

MANNED MISSIONS 1961–64

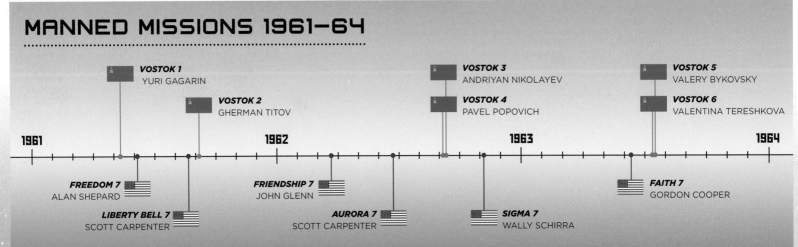

VOSTOK 1
YURI GAGARIN

VOSTOK 2
GHERMAN TITOV

VOSTOK 3
ANDRIYAN NIKOLAYEV

VOSTOK 4
PAVEL POPOVICH

VOSTOK 5
VALERY BYKOVSKY

VOSTOK 6
VALENTINA TERESHKOVA

1961   1962   1963   1964

FREEDOM 7
ALAN SHEPARD

LIBERTY BELL 7
SCOTT CARPENTER

FRIENDSHIP 7
JOHN GLENN

AURORA 7
SCOTT CARPENTER

SIGMA 7
WALLY SCHIRRA

FAITH 7
GORDON COOPER

ORBIT HEATS UP

On 20 February 1962, NASA astronaut John Glenn took off aboard *Mercury* spacecraft *Friendship 7*, which was launched by the powerful *Atlas* rocket. This was a high-risk mission with odds of one-in-six that Glenn would not return. After three successful orbits of Earth, Glenn was told *Friendship 7*'s heat shield may have come loose. Without it, he would burn up during re-entry. Glenn saw flaming chunks flying off *Friendship* as he hurtled towards Earth, but splashed down into the Atlantic unharmed.

⊕ THE FIRST WOMAN IN SPACE, VALENTINA TERESHKOVA FLEW A SOLO MISSION ON *VOSTOK 6* IN 1963.

⊕ JOHN GLENN ENTERING THE *FRIENDSHIP 7* CAPSULE AHEAD OF BECOMING THE FIRST AMERICAN TO ORBIT EARTH.

FEMALE FIRST

Continuing its legacy of space firsts, the Soviet Union launched the first woman into space on 16 June 1963. Cosmonaut Valentina Tereshkova blasted off aboard *Vostok 6* and orbited Earth 48 times over 71 hours. During her mission, Tereshkova was able to talk to cosmonaut Valery Bykovsky who passed by aboard *Vostok 5*. Tereshkova returned unharmed, but a woman would not visit space again for another 19 years.

'We choose to go to the Moon in this decade and do the other things, not because they are easy, but because they are hard...'

KENNEDY'S LUNAR CALLOUT

A year after giving a historic speech to Congress outlining the need for an ambitious space programme, President John F Kennedy made an extraordinary announcement at Rice University on 12 September 1962. He said the US would send men to the Moon and back by the end of the decade.

GROUND CONTROL

Launching each manned or unmanned mission demands thousands of 'invisible' support staff on the ground. These support personnel work tirelessly from huge, complex facilities that contain space-training facilities, mission control centres and launchpads. Their hard work helps ensure the success of many missions.

MAP KEY

- KEY LAUNCH SITES
- HUMANS LAUNCHED INTO ORBIT
- CONTROL AND TRAINING CENTRES
- DEEP-SPACE NETWORK BASES

SPACE CENTRES

Spacecraft are built, maintained and launched from space centres across the world. These are normally located far away from cities for safety or secrecy, but there are other key reasons for where they are built. Cape Canaveral's position benefits from its proximity to the ocean for safe launches and also to the equator, which gives rockets a speed boost.

SPACE AGENCIES

Government-run bodies known as space agencies have been responsible for the majority of space exploration since the mid-20th century. However, in recent years many new space programmes have been financed by private companies, including SpaceX, Virgin and Blue Origin (see p104).

NASA
(NATIONAL AERONAUTICS AND SPACE ADMINISTRATION)
US space agency; founded 1958

GOLDSTONE DEEP SPACE NETWORK
SPACEPORT AMERICA, US
VANDENBERG AIR FORCE STATION, US
WALLOPS FLIGHT FACILITY, US
MADRID DEEP SPACE NETWORK
KENNEDY SPACE CENTER, US
CAPE CANAVERAL AIR FORCE STATION, US
SPACEX ROCKET DEVELOPMENT, US
THE LYNDON B JOHNSON SPACE CENTER, US
GUIANA SPACE CENTRE, FRENCH GUIANA

esa
ESA (EUROPEAN SPACE AGENCY)
Europe's space agency is funded by 22 countries and launches from French Guiana; founded 1975

MANNED MISSIONS

Still very few people have been to space – around 550 in total. The main launch sites for manned missions are the Baikonur Cosmodrome in Kazakhstan (formerly part of the Soviet Union, the land is now leased to and controlled by Russia) and the Kennedy Space Center in the US, from where the *Apollo* and Space Shuttle missions were launched.

THE BAIKONUR COSMODROME IS STILL THE LARGEST LAUNCH FACILITY IN THE WORLD.

ASTRONAUT TRAINING

Before anyone can go to space they have to undergo up to two years of gruelling preparation – it's not simply a case of jumping in a rocket! Astronauts spend time in isolation chambers to get used to how they will live while in space. They also train underwater to help them get used to weightless conditions. Spending up to seven hours underwater, they practise repairing full-size models of spacecraft in a massive, very deep swimming pool.

FREE-FALL TRAINING GIVES ASTRONAUTS THE CHANCE TO EXPERIENCE WEIGHTLESSNESS BEFORE GOING INTO SPACE.

MISSION CONTROL

Manned missions are in constant contact with a mission control centre on the ground. Support personnel in the centre monitor all aspects of the mission, but most of their work is done before the launch as every successful mission requires a huge amount of meticulous planning. Mission control is not always located in the same place as the launch site – US launches take place at Cape Canaveral, Florida, while mission control is 1400km (879 miles) away in Houston, Texas.

PLESETSK
COSMODROME, RUSSIA

THE YURI GAGARIN COSMONAUT
TRAINING CENTRE, RUSSIA

APUSTIN YAR
SMODROME,
RUSSIA

BAIKONUR
COSMODROME, KAZAKHSTAN

JIUQUAN
LAUNCH CENTRE, CHINA

TAIYUAN
LAUNCH CENTRE, CHINA

UCHINOURA
SPACE CENTRE, JAPAN
TANEGASHIMA
SPACE CENTRE, JAPAN

SATISH DHAWAN
SPACE CENTRE, INDIA

XICHANG
LAUNCH CENTRE, CHINA

ROSCOSMOS
Russian space agency; founded in 1992 as the successor to Soviet space programme.

CNSA
(CHINESE NATIONAL SPACE ADMINISTRATION)
China's space agency; founded 1993

CANBERRA
DEEP SPACE NETWORK

THE LYNDON B JOHNSON SPACE CENTER IS MORE POPULARLY KNOWN AS 'HOUSTON' OR 'MISSION CONTROL'.

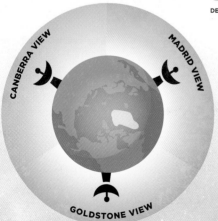

CANBERRA VIEW

MADRID VIEW

GOLDSTONE VIEW

TRACKING SPACECRAFT

There are different ways of following the route of a spacecraft run by various countries. NASA's Deep Space Network uses three communications facilities, each containing an array of vast radio antennae. The three facilities are carefully positioned approximately 120 degrees apart to give 360-degree coverage. This means spacecraft can be tracked constantly.

BEFORE A SPACECRAFT LEAVES THE RANGE OF ONE FACILITY, IT WILL BE PICKED UP BY ANOTHER.

THE TRAVELLER'S GUIDE TO LIVING IN SPACE

Space travel is far from the glamorous experience seen in science-fiction movies. Instead of being bright, light and sparkling white, today's spacecraft can be cramped, claustrophobic and cluttered. What's more, you have to undergo intense training just to survive there. Read on for the revealing truth about living in space.

STRAW-SUCKING SPACE FOOD

Eating and drinking in microgravity is tricky. All of the food has to be prepared in advance and packaged in vacuum bags. This stops any stray crumbs or drops from escaping and getting into the machinery, where they could cause a major malfunction. Often meals are dehydrated and stored in airtight containers waiting for water to be added. You will need to heat these meals in an oven and then suck them up through a straw. Drinks, too, come in plastic bottles with straws.

⊕ EVERYTHING NEEDS TO BE TIED DOWN IN WEIGHTLESS SPACE.

⊕ YOU'LL HAVE TO GET USED TO BRUSHING YOUR TEETH WITH A RINSELESS TOOTHPASTE AND SPITTING IT OUT INTO A TISSUE.

WEIRD WEIGHTLESSNESS

Even for a short three-day journey to the Moon, you will have to get used to the feeling of weightlessness caused by microgravity. You won't be able to drink from a glass or simply put an item down after you've used it. Instead, you'll need to strap your tools onto your belt, drink liquids carefully through a straw and hold onto handles on the wall to stop yourself floating around.

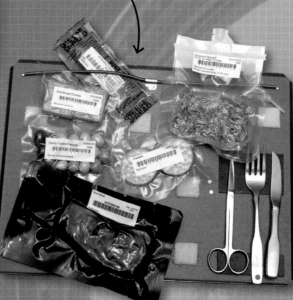

⊕ SPACE FOOD HAS TO BE VACUUM PACKED AND CUTLERY MAGNETISED SO IT DOESN'T FLOAT OFF.

WASHING WITHOUT WATER

There is little water to waste aboard spacecraft and space stations, so you'll keep clean most of the time by wiping yourself with packaged, soapy wipes. The soap is a special space design that dissolves rather than staying sticky. When you do get to have a shower, you'll use a fan to blow the water towards yourself.

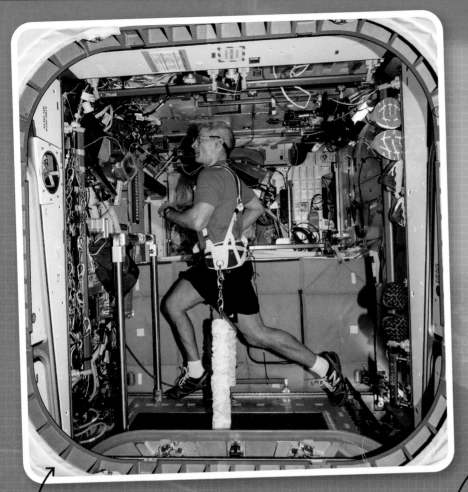

YOU'LL HAVE TO EXERCISE IN SPACE FOR AT LEAST TWO-AND-A-HALF HOURS EVERY DAY TO STAY FIT.

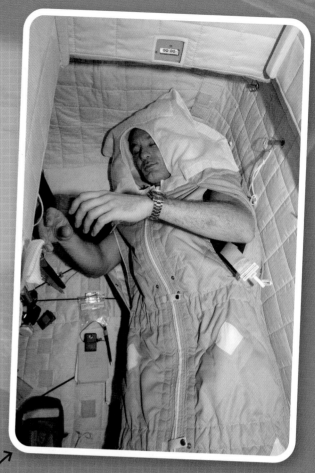

TO SLEEP WELL IN SPACE, WEAR AN EYE MASK AND EARPLUGS TO BLOCK OUT THE HUMMING NOISE OF THE SPACECRAFT.

FEELING FIT

Even if we don't exercise much, Earth's gravity keeps us strong. This is because it pulls on our backs and legs, which means we have to pull the other way to support our weight. But in space there is nothing pulling us down, so our muscles and bones become weaker. This means you'll have to exercise in space on cycling machines and treadmills. Don't be surprised if your face gets puffy over time – being in space can do that.

SLEEPING IN SPACE

One advantage of microgravity is not needing a proper bed. Instead, you'll simply attach your sleeping bag to a wall and climb inside. In some fancy space stations, there might be a cupboard-sized hutch you can sleep in, but get used to having very little privacy! Remember to keep your arms in your sleeping bag while sleeping, or they will rise upwards.

TO USE THE LOO

Believe it or not, you will need to practise to go to the toilet in space. This is because space toilets are like vacuum cleaners that collect the waste that would otherwise float around. You'll urinate down a funnel with suction. For solid waste, you'll have to position yourself over a 10cm (4in) suction hole. When training on Earth, a camera will help you position yourself correctly.

IF YOU'RE OUT ON A SPACEWALK, YOU'LL NEED TO WEAR A SPECIAL NAPPY.

ALWAYS KEEP THE LID DOWN ON A SPACE TOILET.

HISTORY OF SPACESUITS

Spacesuits provide vital protection for astronauts. There are two basic types: spacesuits worn inside spacecraft, and spacesuits worn outside. An outside spacesuit is like a small spacecraft with all of the vital life-support systems needed for survival. Here is how spacesuits have developed over time...

↑ NASA'S FIRST ASTRONAUT CLASS, KNOWN AS THE MERCURY 7.

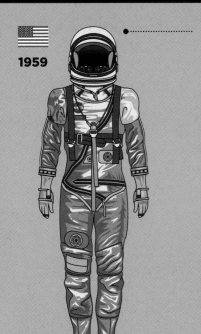

1959

MERCURY SPACESUIT

This spacesuit supplied oxygen to the astronaut and maintained a pressure around their body to keep their exposed fluids (tears, saliva and the moisture on breathing surfaces in the lungs) in a liquid state. This is necessary because above an altitude of around 19km (11 miles) – known as the Armstrong limit – atmospheric pressure is so low that exposed human body fluids begin to boil. Weighing only 10kg (22lb), this was one of the lightest suits ever made.

1965

GEMINI SPACESUIT

The *G4–G7 Gemini* spacesuits were designed for spacewalks, which are also known as extravehicular activities (EVAs). Constructed from six outer layers of nylon and internal layers of polyester, they could withstand temperatures of between -157°C (-314°F) and 121°C (249°F). Life-support systems worn on the front and back of the spacesuit supplied oxygen and hot-and-cold ventilation to the astronaut.

1961

SK-1 SPACESUIT

The Skafandr Kosmicheskiy 1 (*skafandr* is Russian for 'spacesuit') was a basic pressure-suit worn by Yuri Gagarin and other early cosmonauts on the *Vostok* missions. The bright-orange nylon suit had a visored helmet, an inner pressure liner with communication hoses, and a mirror on its sleeve for looking at difficult-to-see gauges and switches.

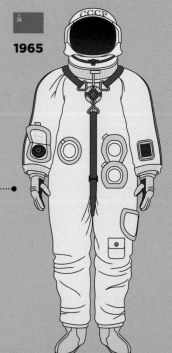

1965

VOSKHOD SPACESUIT

The Berkut (Russian for 'golden eagle') was the spacesuit worn by *Voskhod 2* cosmonaut Alexei Leonov during the first ever spacewalk (see p32). Oxygen for 45 minutes was supplied via a metal backpack. A relief valve allowed oxygen, carbon dioxide, heat and moisture to be released into space. The valve saved Leonov's life when his spacesuit ballooned. Leonov used the valve to deflate the suit enough to re-enter the spacecraft.

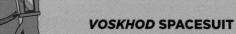

DRESSED TO IMPRESS

Spacesuits can look quite chunky. This is because they are made from up to 16 layers, including:

OUTER LAYER IS A COMBINATION OF TOUGH MATERIALS, SUCH AS BULLETPROOF KEVLAR, TEFLON AND NOMEX

MANY LAYERS OF INSULATION TO KEEP A CONSTANT TEMPERATURE AND PROTECT THE ASTRONAUT FROM BEING HURT BY OBJECTS

RIPSTOP LINER TO PREVENT DAMAGE TO THE LAYERS BENEATH

RESTRAINT LAYER TO KEEP THE 'BLADDER' LAYER IN THE RIGHT SHAPE

BLADDER LAYER THAT MAINTAINS THE CORRECT PRESSURE FOR THE HUMAN BODY AND HOLDS OXYGEN

SET OF LAYERS THAT FORMS THE INNER LIQUID COOLING AND VENTILATION GARMENT

LAYERS OF PROTECTION

WATER TUBES

PARTS OF A SPACESUIT

GOLD-COATED VISOR TO PROTECT AGAINST THE SUN'S RAYS

PORTABLE LIFE SUPPORT SYSTEM

TEMPERATURE CONTROL

HEATED GLOVES

APOLLO SPACESUIT

1966

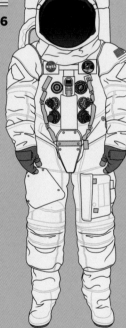

The *Apollo* spacesuit had to provide enough flexibility to walk on the Moon's surface. The spacesuit was made up of several layers, including an internal layer with tubes of liquid to cool the astronaut down. Moonboots consisted of an overshoe and inner boot, and thick gloves were individually moulded to each astronaut's hands with rubber fingertips to grip objects. The Portable Life Support System was the spacesuit's backpack containing oxygen, water and radio equipment.

FEITIAN SPACESUIT

2008

The Feitian (Mandarin for 'flying in the sky') suit was designed for spacewalks on the Chinese *Shenzhou* mission. Modelled after the one-piece Russian Orlan-M spacesuit, the Feitian was a one-size-fits-all suit made of a light, synthetic fibre that protected wearers from extreme heat and cold. The outer layers of the suit could withstand impact from floating rock particles, known as micro-meteoroids, in space.

1994

2020

SPACE SHUTTLE SUIT

Fondly known as the 'Pumpkin Suit' because of its colour, the Advanced Crew Escape Space Suit System (ACES) was designed to provide an Earth-like environment for astronauts during launch and re-entry, and protection during an emergency. It was adapted from high-altitude flying suits used by the US Air Force and carried 10 minutes of emergency oxygen.

THE Z-2 SPACESUIT

The Z-2 is a prototype that an astronaut puts on by climbing in through a hatch in its back. With life-support systems, flexible fabric and a large bubble helmet, it is designed for both spacewalks and walking on the surfaces of planets. This makes it different from most other outside spacesuits, which are mainly designed for spacewalks. The Z-2 is just a prototype, but NASA hopes it will be rolled out for spacewalk missions in the mid-2020s.

SPACEWALKERS

A spacewalk, or extravehicular activity (EVA), is when an astronaut puts on a protective spacesuit and leaves their spacecraft to enter the vacuum of space. Astronauts go on spacewalks to conduct experiments, test equipment, or repair their spacecraft.

In 1965, Russian Alexei Leonov became the first person to go on a spacewalk, which lasted for 10 minutes. Today's spacewalkers use a tether to stay attached to their spacecraft, but a few 20th-century astronauts used a backpack with simple thrusters to stop them floating away. Astronauts train for spacewalks in swimming pools because the body 'floats' in both situations. The Russian Anatoly Solovyev holds the record for most time spacewalking at 82 hours.

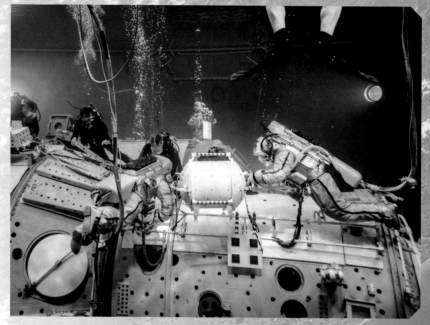

⬆ COSMONAUTS TRAINING UNDERWATER AT THE YURI GAGARIN TRAINING CENTRE IN MOSCOW.

FAMOUS SPACEWALKERS

ALEXEI LEONOV (1965)
ALEXEI LEONOV FAMOUSLY MADE THE FIRST SPACEWALK FROM *VOSKHOD 2* IN 1965. BUT THINGS NEARLY TURNED OUT VERY BADLY (see p30).

ALFRED WORDEN (1971)
APOLLO 15 ASTRONAUT ALFRED WORDEN MADE THE FIRST SPACEWALK IN DEEP SPACE. HE DID THIS BY EXITING THE LUNAR COMMAND AND SERVICE MODULE AT AROUND 275,000km (170,000 miles) FROM EARTH.

BRUCE MCCANDLESS (1984)
SPACE SHUTTLE ASTRONAUT BRUCE MCCANDLESS MADE THE FIRST UNTETHERED SPACEWALK. MCCANDLESS STAYED CLOSE TO THE SHUTTLE BY USING A 'MANNED MANEUVERING UNIT' (MMU), A BACKPACK POWERED BY GAS THRUSTERS.

ED WHITE (1965)
ED WHITE MADE AMERICA'S FIRST SPACEWALK IN 1965, 15 DAYS AFTER RUSSIAN ALEXEI LEONOV. WHITE'S SPACEWALK LASTED FOR 20 MINUTES.

SVETLANA SAVITSKAYA (1984)
SVETLANA SAVITSKAYA BECAME THE FIRST WOMAN TO GO ON A SPACEWALK. SHE DID THIS WHEN SHE EXITED THE *SALYUT 7* SPACE STATION FOR A WELDING EXPERIMENT OUTSIDE.

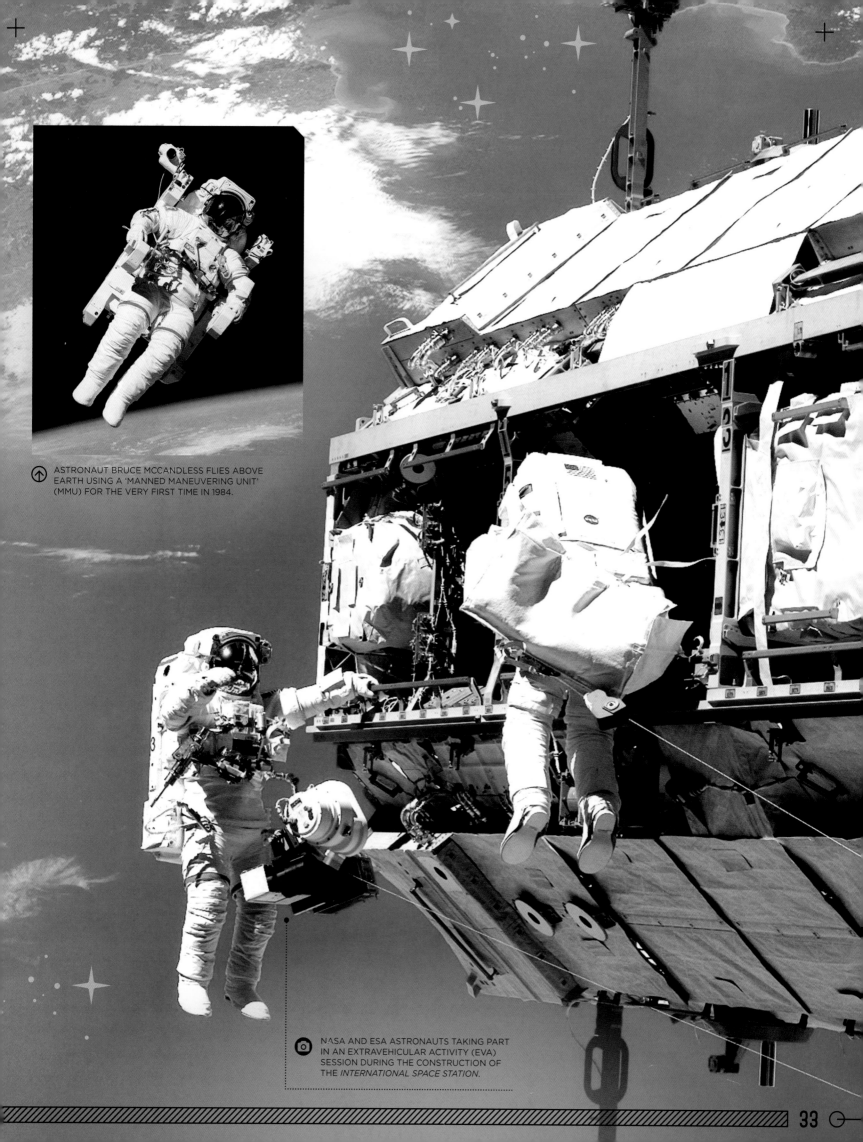

ASTRONAUT BRUCE MCCANDLESS FLIES ABOVE EARTH USING A 'MANNED MANEUVERING UNIT' (MMU) FOR THE VERY FIRST TIME IN 1984.

NASA AND ESA ASTRONAUTS TAKING PART IN AN EXTRAVEHICULAR ACTIVITY (EVA) SESSION DURING THE CONSTRUCTION OF THE *INTERNATIONAL SPACE STATION*.

The moon missions

On 16 July 1969, the *Apollo 11* Moon mission blasted off from the Kennedy Space Center, Florida. The US was just 384,000km (238,600 miles) from putting the first people on the Moon...

THE LUNAR LANDER

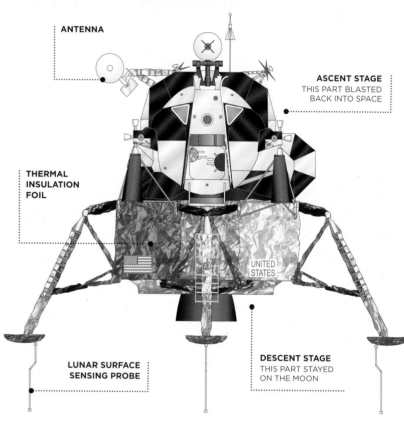

ANTENNA

ASCENT STAGE
THIS PART BLASTED BACK INTO SPACE

THERMAL INSULATION FOIL

UNITED STATES

LUNAR SURFACE SENSING PROBE

DESCENT STAGE
THIS PART STAYED ON THE MOON

⤒ EDWIN 'BUZZ' ALDRIN, THE SECOND PERSON TO WALK ON THE MOON, 20 JULY 1969.

⊛ CLOSE UP OF THE BOOTPRINT LEFT BY ONE OF THE FIRST STEPS ON THE MOON.

LUNAR LANDING

On 20 July, astronaut Neil Armstrong searched desperately for a spot to land on the surface of the Moon. The lunar lander carrying Armstrong and Buzz Aldrin had only 60 seconds' worth of fuel left. The tension was terrible. Half a billion people watching the Moon landing on television held their breath. Then Armstrong's voice crackled over the radio: 'The Eagle has landed.' Humans were safely on the Moon.

GIANT STEPS

As Neil Armstrong descended onto the Moon's surface, he uttered the now-famous words: 'That's one small step for [a] man, one giant leap for mankind.' The Moon revealed itself to be bleak and lonely with no sign of life. The astronauts set up experiments, took photographs and collected rocks. They discovered the lunar surface was covered in a fine, grey dust that smelled like gunpowder and clung to everything it touched. Finally, the astronauts planted a flag on the surface and returned home. The mission was over.

HOUSTON, WE'VE HAD A PROBLEM

The *Apollo* space programme lasted from 1961 to 1972 during which time there were several named missions. *Apollo* missions 1 to 10 were test missions (2 and 3 were assigned numbers, but never took place). *Apollo 12* was another successful Moon mission, but disaster struck with *Apollo 13*. Fifty-six hours into the voyage, one of the oxygen tanks blew up and the other failed. Mission control suggested the *Apollo 13* astronauts seal themselves in the lunar module to preserve power and oxygen. This saved their lives. After a daring slingshot manoeuvre around the Moon, *Apollo 13* returned safely to Earth.

THE *APOLLO 13* FLIGHT DIRECTORS CELEBRATE THE MOMENT THAT COMMAND MODULE *ODYSSEY* SPLASHES DOWN BACK ON EARTH.

THE *APOLLO 15* LRV TRAVELLED A TOTAL OF 27km (17 miles) OVER THREE HOURS.

OVER AND OUT

Landing on 11 December 1972, *Apollo 17* was the last manned mission to the Moon. It included the first astronaut-scientist, Harrison Schmitt, who set up experiments to measure possible earthquake activity and explore some of the Moon's meteor strikes. However, at an estimated cost of USD$25 billion (around $175 billion today), the *Apollo* missions were too expensive to continue. The Moon has not been visited by humans since.

LUNAR ROVER

The 1971 *Apollo 15* mission was a major advance on its predecessors because it included a Lunar Roving Vehicle (LRV). This was a wheeled 'Moon buggy' that could transport the astronauts much further distances to collect greater quantities of rock. One such rock, nicknamed the 'genesis rock', was discovered to be 4 billion years old. The LRV was such a success that subsequent rovers were included on the *Apollo 16* and *17* Moon missions.

MORE THAN 110kg (240lb) OF MOON ROCK WAS GATHERED BY THE *APOLLO 17* ASTRONAUTS. SOME OF IT REMAINS SEALED, READY TO BE ANALYSED AT A LATER DATE.

TO THE MOON AND BACK

The *Apollo 11* mission to transport men to the Moon and back required a series of complex, perfectly timed manoeuvres to be performed in space. Each mission began with the launch of a three-stage *Saturn V* – the most powerful rocket ever constructed.

ROUTE TO THE MOON

1 LIFT OFF

THE *SATURN V* ROCKET CARRYING *APOLLO 11* BLASTS OFF AT 8.32am LOCAL TIME, TRAVELLING AT 9920km/h (6164mph) .

2 STAGE ONE

AFTER TWO MINUTES AND 44 SECONDS, *APOLLO 11* HAS REACHED A HEIGHT OF AROUND 68km (42 miles). *SATURN V*'S STAGE ONE ROCKET FALLS AWAY AND STAGE TWO FIRES UP.

3 STAGE TWO

THE FIVE ENGINES ON STAGE TWO FIRE FOR AROUND EIGHT MINUTES BEFORE FALLING AWAY. THIS HAS TAKEN THE SPACECRAFT INTO EARTH'S UPPER ATMOSPHERE.

4 STAGE THREE

A SINGLE ENGINE FIRES *APOLLO 11* INTO EARTH'S ORBIT. IT IS NOW 11 MINUTES AND 42 SECONDS SINCE LAUNCH.

5 IN ORBIT

APOLLO 11 SHUTS DOWN ITS STAGE-THREE ENGINE AS IT ORBITS THE EARTH ONE-AND-A-HALF TIMES.

6 TRANSLUNAR INJECTION

STAGE THREE'S ENGINE FIRES AGAIN TO BLAST *APOLLO 11* OUT OF EARTH'S ORBIT AND TOWARDS THE MOON.

7 SEPARATION, EXTRACTION AND DOCKING

THE COMMAND AND SERVICE MODULE (CSM) SEPARATES FROM STAGE THREE, ROTATES 180 DEGREES AND DOCKS WITH THE LUNAR MODULE (LM) STILL IN STAGE THREE. THE CSM THEN PULLS THE LM AWAY FROM STAGE THREE, WHICH FALLS AWAY.

12 SEPARATION AND RE-ENTRY

BEFORE RE-ENTRY INTO EARTH'S ATMOSPHERE, THE CSM SEPARATES. THE SERVICE MODULE IS JETTISONED AND THE COMMAND MODULE CONTAINING THE ASTRONAUTS HURTLES TOWARDS EARTH.

13 SPLASHDOWN

FIRST AT 7.3km (4.5 miles), AND THEN AT 3km (1.8 miles) ABOVE EARTH'S SURFACE, PARACHUTES ARE DEPLOYED. THE CM THEN SPLASHES DOWN INTO THE ATLANTIC OCEAN. MISSION OVER!

8 MOON'S ORBIT

TOGETHER, THE CSM AND LM FORM THE FINAL SPACECRAFT, WHICH FLIES TO THE MOON OVER THE NEXT THREE DAYS. THE SPACECRAFT THEN ENTERS THE MOON'S ORBIT AND SEPARATES AGAIN.

9 LUNAR LANDING

ASTRONAUTS NEIL ARMSTRONG AND BUZZ ALDRIN FLY TO THE LUNAR SURFACE IN THE LM WHILE MICHAEL COLLINS STAYS IN ORBIT ABOARD THE CSM.

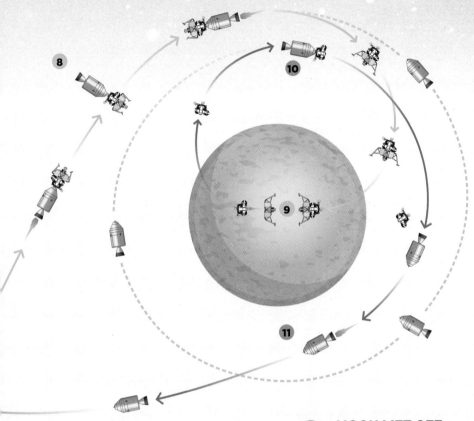

SATURN V

The 111m (364ft) tall, 2.8 million kg (6.1 million lb) *Saturn V* rocket was made up of three smaller rockets called stages that gave it the necessary thrust to first go into orbit around Earth and then head towards the Moon. After each stage had burnt through its fuel of kerosene, liquid hydrogen and liquid oxygen, it would fall away and the next stage would take over.

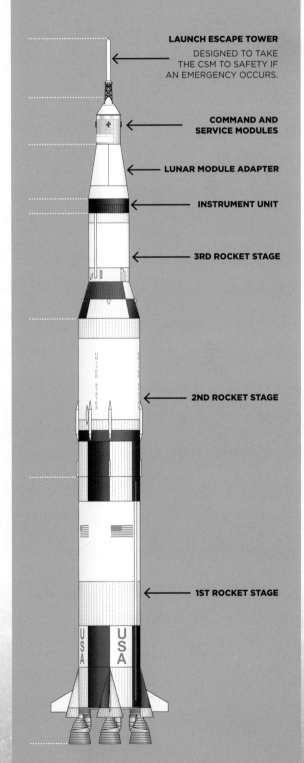

LAUNCH ESCAPE TOWER
DESIGNED TO TAKE THE CSM TO SAFETY IF AN EMERGENCY OCCURS.

COMMAND AND SERVICE MODULES

LUNAR MODULE ADAPTER

INSTRUMENT UNIT

3RD ROCKET STAGE

2ND ROCKET STAGE

1ST ROCKET STAGE

11 TRANS EARTH INJECTION

THE CSM FIRES ITS ROCKET TO BLAST OUT OF THE MOON'S ORBIT AND TOWARDS EARTH. IT IS NOW HOMEWARD BOUND.

10 MOON LIFT OFF

THE LM'S ASCENT STAGE (TOP HALF) BLASTS AWAY FROM ITS DESCENT STAGE (BOTTOM HALF, WHICH STAYS ON THE MOON) AND DOCKS WITH THE CSM. THE ASTRONAUTS RE-ENTER THE CSM. THE LM IS THEN JETTISONED.

COMMAND AND SERVICE MODULE (CSM)

COMMAND MODULE

SERVICE MODULE

LUNAR MODULE (LM)

ASCENT STAGE

DESCENT STAGE

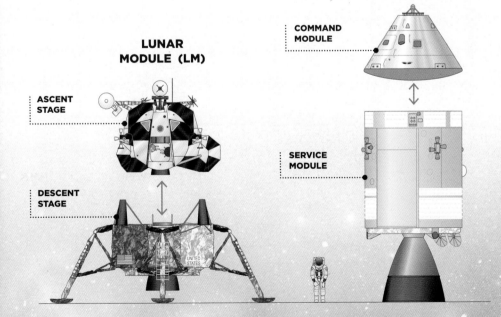

THE TRAVELLER'S GUIDE TO THE MOON

Travelling to the Moon is a good choice. Why? Because it is a tried-and-tested option. Neil Armstrong was the first person to set foot on the Moon over 50 years ago. Now a total of 12 astronauts have been there, but none since 1972. Why don't you become number 13?

LANDING

The Moon isn't far from Earth at around 385,000km (239,000 miles) away. However, you'll still need a rocket such as a *Saturn V* to carry the 4.3 million litres (950,000 gallons) of fuel needed to get you there. The *Apollo* missions used a lunar lander to touch down on the Moon, so you'll need some practice for this on Earth. The good news is that the Moon's surface is not yet covered by buildings, so there are plenty of places to land.

KIT BOX

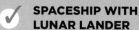

- ✓ **SPACESHIP WITH LUNAR LANDER**
- ✓ **A PORTABLE LIFE SUPPORT SYSTEM BACKPACK**
- ✓ **A GOLD-PLATED HELMET VISOR**

SURFACE

The Moon is a barren, rocky place pockmarked by craters and covered with a fine, grey dust the consistency of talcum powder. It sticks to everything, so don't get upset if it dirties your spacesuit. It's important your suit contains both heating and cooling systems – the temperature can swing wildly from a chilling -233°C (-387°F) to a blistering 122°C (253°F)! Also, remember to fit your helmet with both a sun shield and a gold-plated visor; otherwise sunburn and potential sun blindness can be a real problem during the day.

EXPLORING

A bulky lunar backpack is officially called the Portable Life Support System (PLSS). The name is fitting: the backpack contains oxygen, cooling and heating systems, plus radio equipment. On Earth, the backpack weighs 163kg (359lb), but on the Moon, where gravity is one sixth of that on Earth, it weighs just 27kg (59lb). This low gravity will make long lunar jumps a fun reality. If you get tired of walking, hop into one of the lunar rovers left behind by the *Apollo* missions. Just don't drive into any large craters!

THE MOON DATA FILE

average **150 million km** (93 million miles) *from the Sun.*

THE SUN ◎ MOON MERCURY VENUS EARTH MARS JUPITER SATURN URANUS NEPTUNE

SIZE AND DISTANCE NOT TO SCALE

TEMPERATURE

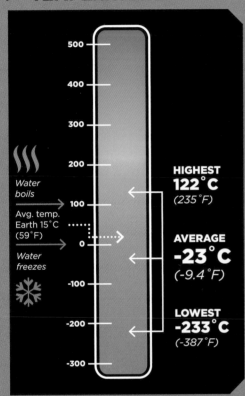

500
400
300
200
100
0
-100
-200
-300

Water boils

Avg. temp. Earth 15°C (59°F)

Water freezes

HIGHEST
122°C
(235°F)

AVERAGE
-23°C
(-9.4°F)

LOWEST
-233°C
(-387°F)

SIZE

THE MOON   EARTH

AVERAGE DIAMETER
3475km
(2159 miles)

The Moon is 385,000km (239,000 miles) from Earth on average. It is slowly moving away at roughly 4cm (1.5in) every year.

SPEED

1km/sec
(0.62 miles/sec)

Speed the Moon orbits Earth.

EARTH: 30km/sec (18.5 miles/sec)
Speed the Earth orbits the Sun.

CALENDAR

Length of a day
29.5 Earth days

Time to orbit Earth
27.3 Earth days

SURFACE CHARACTER

EXOSPHERE:

There is no atmosphere on the Moon, so footprints can remain there for decades.

Because there is no atmosphere to spread light around, the sky appears black.

GRAVITY:

x 0.17
of EARTH

If you weigh 70kg (11st) on Earth, you will weigh just 12kg (2st) on the Moon.

SURFACE AREA:

The Moon's surface area is 38 million sq km (14.6 million sq miles) – roughly the size of Asia.

The Moon's diameter is a bit bigger than the length of Africa.

SPOTLIGHT

LUNAR MYSTERY

The US flag planted on the Moon in 1969 was designed to support itself, as shown below. However, there is no wind, rain or any other weather on the Moon, so the flag can't flutter.

modern moon missions

The *Apollo 17* mission marked the last time humans set foot on the Moon. Since then several governments have revealed plans for a lunar return. Their ideas include space stations that stay in the Moon's orbit and a permanent human base on its surface.

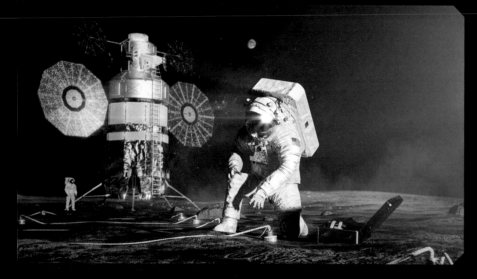

ARTEMIS AIMS HIGH

In 2019, NASA announced its *Artemis* programme to send astronauts to the Moon by 2024. The *Space Launch System* (*SLS*) rocket will launch the astronauts aboard an *Orion* spacecraft, which will then dock with a space station called *Gateway* in orbit around the Moon. From *Gateway*, astronauts will launch mini-missions to the Moon's surface to search for water and mineral resources. Missions will last 30 to 90 days and include female and male astronauts.

THIS ARTIST'S IMPRESSION SHOWS ASTRONAUTS TAKING PART IN THE *ARTEMIS* PROGRAMME, WHICH NASA HOPES WILL BE PART OF A WIDER PROJECT TO SEND MANNED MISSIONS TO MARS.

CHANDRAYAAN'S CONTROLLED CRASHES

In 2008, India entered the world of space exploration with a controlled crash-landing of its *Chandrayaan-1* probe onto the Moon. Once there, the probe found evidence of water molecules in the lunar soil near the Moon's south pole. The find led to the launch of *Chandrayaan-2*, a spacecraft that dropped a lander onto the Moon in September 2019. India's space plans do not end there: a *Chandrayaan-3* mission to test out new space technologies for humans has been announced for 2024.

THE *CHANDRAYAAN* MISSIONS MADE INDIA THE FOURTH COUNTRY TO MAKE A SOFT-LANDING ON THE MOON, AFTER THE US, CHINA AND RUSSIA.

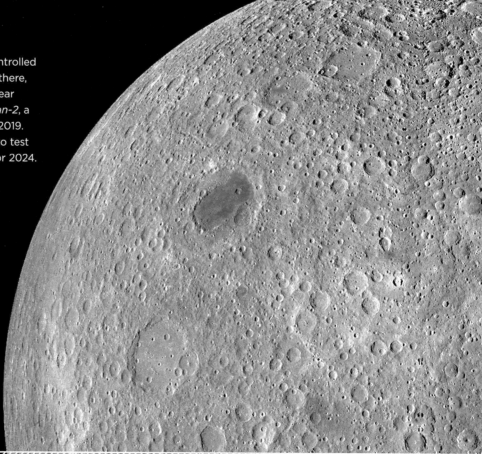

 THE *YUTU 2* ROVER LEAVING THE *CHANG'E 4* LUNAR LANDER TO EXPLORE THE SURFACE OF THE MOON.

FAR-SIDE ROVING

In January 2019, China made space history by becoming the first nation to land a rover on the far side of the Moon. After leaving its *Chang'e 4* lunar lander, the *Yutu 2* rover began exploring the surface. The purpose of the mission was to take soil tests to uncover the origins of water on the Moon. We know little about the far side of the Moon, which stays permanently out of view of Earth. This is because the Moon spins on its axis at the same rate that it orbits the planet.

THE FAR SIDE OF THE MOON IS MORE POCKMARKED WITH CRATERS THAN ITS FACING SIDE, WHICH HAS INTRIGUED ASTRONOMERS.

A permanent space station on the Moon is being developed by the European Space Agency (ESA). The base would be constructed using inflatable domes for workspaces, laboratories and homes. Robots would then build a protective shell over the village to stop it from being damaged by meteorites and harmful radiation. The village would be constructed at the lunar south pole, which gets year-round sunlight. This sunlight would power the village's solar panels and help plants grow in its greenhouses.

THE LUNAR VILLAGE'S INFLATABLE DOMES WOULD BE LINKED BY PRESSURISED WALKWAYS AND AIRLOCKS.

RARE RESOURCES

For years, the Moon appeared to be a lifeless world with little to offer humans. But underneath the surface, it has many resources that can help support life. The discovery of water is perhaps the most important. Split into its two chemical components – hydrogen and oxygen – water can provide air to breathe and propellant for space rockets. The Moon can also be mined for its many mineral resources. These include titanium, gold, iron and the chemical helium-3, which could provide power for nuclear reactors.

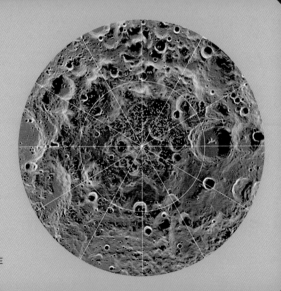

THIS INFRARED IMAGE TAKEN BY THE *CHANDRAYAAN 1* PROBE SHOWS WATER MOLECULES ON THE MOON'S SURFACE.

HISTORY OF ROCKETS

Rocket technology has come a long way since Robert Goddard's rocket in 1926 (see p13). Modern, multi-stage rockets carry probes, orbiters and landers to other planets in our Solar System. Today, rockets are being developed to transport people to the Moon, Mars and maybe beyond.

AN *ARIANE 5* ROCKET LAUNCHING *TERRESTAR-1*, THE HEAVIEST-EVER COMMERCIAL SATELLITE ON 1 JUNE 2009.

ARIANE 5

Based on the European Space Agency's 1979 *Ariane 1*, *Ariane 5* is a heavy-lift rocket that typically carries payloads such as satellites into Earth's orbit. Unlike its predecessors, which had stacked stages, *Ariane 5* carries booster rockets on either side of its central core. *Ariane 5* was the first European rocket to use cryogenic propellants, which have to be stored at low temperatures.

R-7

Based on the *V-2* technology developed by the Nazis, the *R-7* was the brainchild of Soviet chief rocket designer, Sergei Korolev. Instead of being stacked in stages, the *R-7* used a cluster of rocket stages grouped around a central core. Operational between 1957 and 1968, the *R-7* fired *Sputnik 1* into space (see p16) and was used as the model for the later *Soyuz* family of launchers, which became the most widely used rockets in the world.

FROM LITTLE TO LARGE, A RANGE OF ROCKETS FROM HISTORY.

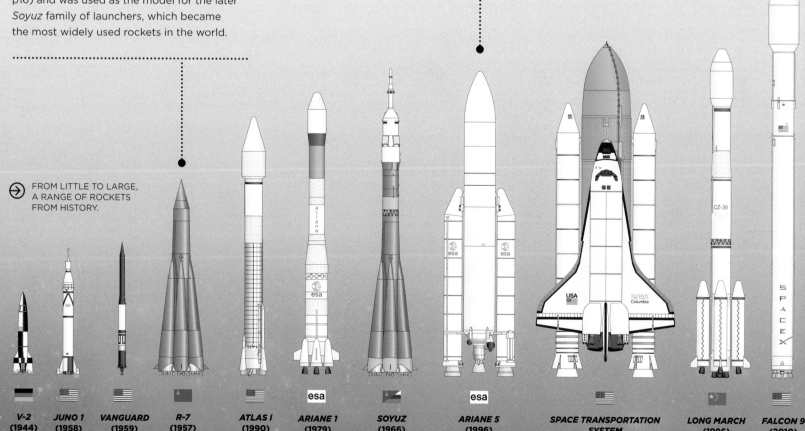

| V-2 (1944) | JUNO 1 (1958) | VANGUARD (1959) | R-7 (1957) | ATLAS I (1990) | ARIANE 1 (1979) | SOYUZ (1966) | ARIANE 5 (1996) | SPACE TRANSPORTATION SYSTEM (1981) | LONG MARCH (1996) | FALCON 9 (2010) |

FALCON HEAVY

Built by the private US company SpaceX, the *Falcon Heavy* is the most powerful operational rocket in the world. Capable of carrying a payload of 58 tonnes (57 tons), it features a central first stage with booster rockets on either side. The *Falcon Heavy* carries heavy satellites into Earth's orbit and is notable because all three of its first stages guide themselves back to Earth after being jettisoned (see p45). These stages can then be used again on future flights.

NEW GLENN ROCKET

Named after the first US astronaut in orbit, John Glenn, the *New Glenn* rocket is scheduled for its first flight in the 2020s. Designed to carry a payload of 57 tonnes (56 tons), it is a heavy-lift rocket with a first stage that can be reused up to 25 times. The rocket is built by the private company Blue Origin and will be used to transport people and payloads into Earth's orbit.

THE *SPACE LAUNCH SYSTEM*

Designed to be the most powerful rocket yet built, NASA's *Space Launch System* (*SLS*) is being developed to transport astronauts to the Moon, Mars and one day even deep space. Scheduled to be unveiled in the 2020s, the *SLS* can change to fit specific missions. Its core stage will remain constant for each mission, but an upper stage and booster rockets can be added to achieve greater distances. It is the rocket that will next carry US astronauts to the Moon in 2024.

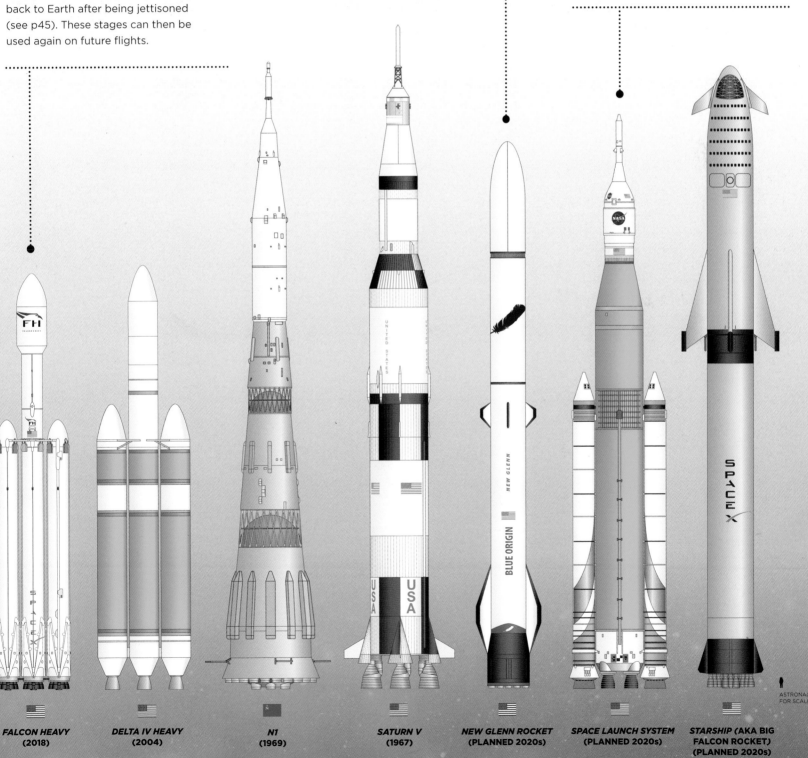

ASTRONAUT FOR SCALE

FALCON HEAVY (2018)

DELTA IV HEAVY (2004)

N1 (1969)

SATURN V (1967)

NEW GLENN ROCKET (PLANNED 2020s)

SPACE LAUNCH SYSTEM (PLANNED 2020s)

STARSHIP (AKA BIG FALCON ROCKET) (PLANNED 2020s)

REUSABLE SPACECRAFT

Exploring space is expensive. During the Space Race, billions were spent on building and launching spacecraft that could be used only once. In the 1980s, NASA unveiled a winged spaceplane that could be reused: the Space Shuttle. Today, reusable technology is leading the way in spacecraft design.

SPACE SHUTTLE *ENDEAVOUR* APPROACHING THE *INTERNATIONAL SPACE STATION* IN 2008 WITH ITS PAYLOAD DOORS OPEN REVEALING A CONTAINER OF SUPPLIES.

REUSING THE SPACE SHUTTLE

The Space Transportation System, commonly known as the Space Shuttle, was a group of five reusable spaceplanes that operated from 1981 to 2011. They blasted into space using an external fuel tank and two booster rockets, which fell away when the shuttle reached Earth's orbit, leaving it to depend on its own engines and fuel supply to land. This it did on a landing strip in the same way as an aeroplane.

THE SPACE SHUTTLE

SPACE SHUTTLE *ATLANTIS* LAUNCHING FOR THE FIRST TIME IN 1985.

CANADARM

The shuttle had a 15m (50ft) robotic arm called Canadarm (it was provided by the Canadian government). The arm had six moveable joints and was hollow inside. On Earth, Canadarm wouldn't support its own weight, but in space it could lift loads of over 265,000kg (582,000lb).

CREW QUARTERS

In front of the payload bay were the shuttle's flight deck and mid-deck. The flight deck looked like that of a high-tech aeroplane, with two seats for the mission commander and pilot and a large instrument panel in front. Directly behind the flight deck was the mid-deck, where the astronauts worked, ate, slept and washed in the personal hygiene station.

SPACE RIDER

A reusable spacecraft that can stay in orbit for two months at a time to conduct scientific experiments is set to take flight in 2022. The European Space Agency's *Space Rider* will launch aboard a *Vega-C* rocket and can carry payloads of up to 800kg (1760lb) in its cargo bay. *Space Rider* will return to Earth by firing its retro-thrusters and then gliding down to a landing strip using a large, parafoil parachute.

AN ARTIST'S REPRESENTATION OF THE STAGES OF *SPACE RIDER*.

PAYLOAD BAY

Large payloads such as satellites, telescopes and space-station modules were transported into orbit inside the shuttle's large payload bay. Once in space, the hinged payload doors would open to release the cargo.

REUSABLE ROCKETS

The SpaceX company has a range of reusable rockets that it operates. On a test misson in 2018, a *Falcon Heavy* rocket put a car into orbit around the Sun. The company also has plans for a highly ambitious reusable spacecraft that can transport 100 people and 136 tonnes (133.8 tons) of supplies to Mars. The ultimate goal of the *Starship*, as it has been called, is to colonise Mars with humans sometime in the future.

SPACE SHUTTLE *ATLANTIS* BEING SLOWED BY ITS DRAG CHUTE UPON LANDING IN 1994.

TWO *FALCON HEAVY* BOOSTER ROCKETS LANDING VERTICALLY AFTER A LAUNCH AT KENNEDY SPACE CENTER ON 6 FEBRUARY 2018.

SPACE STATIONS

After the success of the US *Apollo* missions, the Soviet Union gave up its plan to land a man on the Moon. Instead it turned its attention to launching space probes and building space stations.

Designed to stay in orbit around Earth, space stations are used to conduct experiments and observe how the human body reacts to long periods in space. The Soviet Union led the way with space-station technology, launching seven *Salyut* stations between 1971 and 1982. The largest and longest-lasting space station, however, was a joint effort between several nations. A permanently manned satellite around Earth, the *International Space Station* (*ISS*) launched its first module in 1998. Today, the *ISS* stands as a testament to an era of multi-national cooperation in space.

THE INTERNATIONAL SPACE STATION

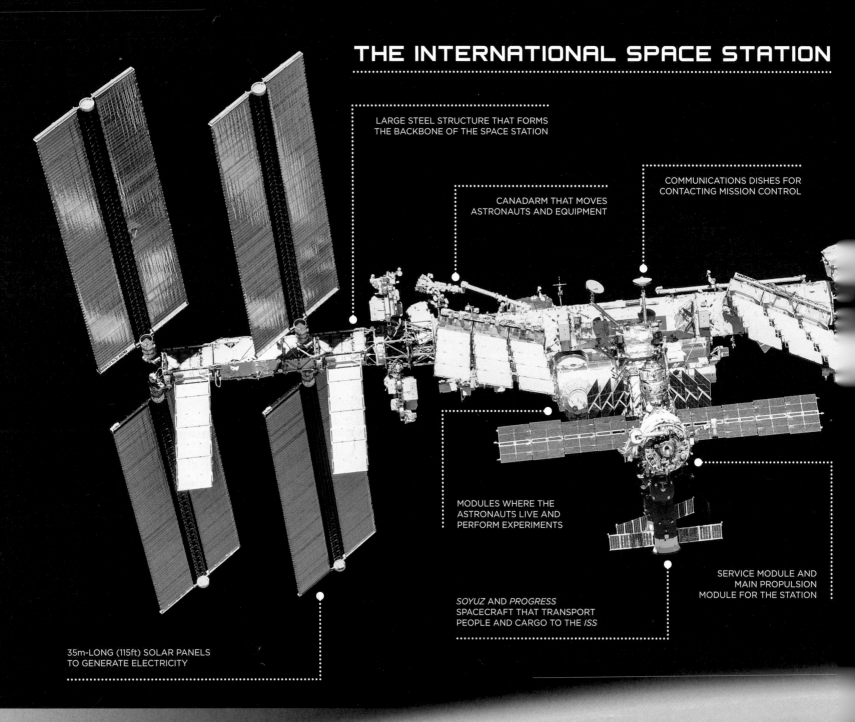

LARGE STEEL STRUCTURE THAT FORMS THE BACKBONE OF THE SPACE STATION

COMMUNICATIONS DISHES FOR CONTACTING MISSION CONTROL

CANADARM THAT MOVES ASTRONAUTS AND EQUIPMENT

MODULES WHERE THE ASTRONAUTS LIVE AND PERFORM EXPERIMENTS

SERVICE MODULE AND MAIN PROPULSION MODULE FOR THE STATION

SOYUZ AND *PROGRESS* SPACECRAFT THAT TRANSPORT PEOPLE AND CARGO TO THE *ISS*

35m-LONG (115ft) SOLAR PANELS TO GENERATE ELECTRICITY

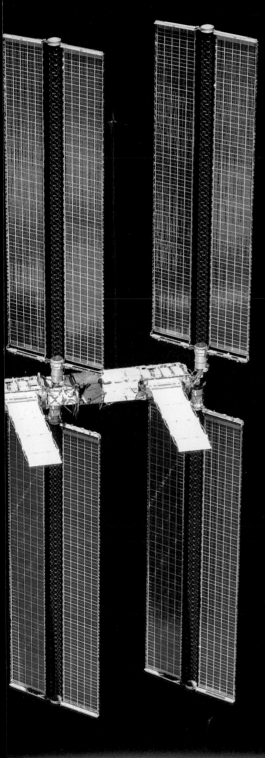

THE *INTERNATIONAL SPACE STATION* ON 4 OCTOBER 2018, AS VIEWED FROM A *SOYUZ* SPACECRAFT TAKING ASTRONAUTS HOME AFTER SPENDING 197 DAYS IN SPACE.

SPACE STATIONS

SALYUT 1 (1971)

Salyut 1 could house three cosmonauts in three pressurised compartments. It orbited Earth almost 3000 times and spent 175 days in space. Six more *Salyuts* were launched, with the last, *Salyut 7*, orbiting Earth between 1982 and 1986.

SALYUT 1

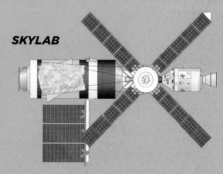

ASTRONAUT FOR SCALE

SKYLAB (1973–1979)

America's *Skylab* stayed in space for six years to conduct experiments on weightlessness. The longest mission lasted for three months.

SKYLAB

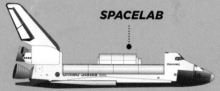

esa SPACELAB (1983–1998)

Spacelab was Europe's contribution to space-station technology. It was designed to carry out experiments in zero gravity. Strictly speaking it was not a space station, but a science lab within the Space Shuttle.

SPACELAB

MIR (1986–2000)

The Soviet *Mir* was the largest space station built at the time and the first to be permanently occupied. Cosmonaut Valeri Polyakov stayed aboard *Mir* for 437 days, breaking the record for the longest stay in space.

MIR

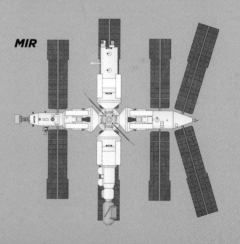

THE *ISS* (1998–)

Covering the size of a football field, the *ISS* is made up of 16 modules: five provided by Russia, eight by America, two by Japan, and one by Europe. It is powered by over 2500 sq metres (27,000 sq ft) of solar panels that convert sunlight to electricity.

SPACE STATION SIZE CHART

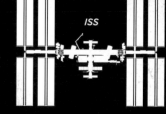

SKYLAB

SPACE SHUTTLE

ISS

EXPLORING THE SOLAR SYSTEM

In the last 60 years of space exploration, humans have ventured no further than our Moon. Instead, robotic spacecraft known as probes have been sent to explore the different planets and objects that make up our Solar System and beyond. Able to operate in environments hostile to humans, probes have beamed back data and photos revealing worlds previously unseen.

SPACECRAFT TYPES

These are some of the main types of spacecraft that have been sent on journeys of discovery across the Solar System.

FLYBY SPACECRAFT
These pass by objects, such as moons and planets, recording data as they go, before heading off elsewhere.

ORBITERS
These go into orbit around a body, making detailed studies from high above the surface.

ENTRY PROBES/IMPACTORS/LANDERS
Entry probes descend into a body's atmosphere and usually work for just a short time. Landers and impactors touch down on the surface. All record data about their surroundings.

ROVERS
These are moving vehicles that travel (slowly) across the surface of other worlds to explore them.

MANNED MISSIONS
So far, manned missions have visited just one Solar System body, the Moon.

EARTH

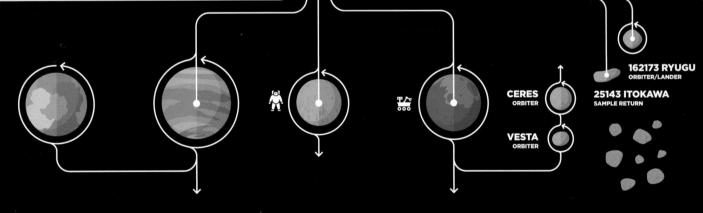

CERES ORBITER

VESTA ORBITER

162173 RYUGU ORBITER/LANDER

25143 ITOKAWA SAMPLE RETURN

THE SUN

20 x ORBITERS

NOTABLE SPACECRAFT

1974 *HELIOS 1* orbiter
1994 *ULYSSES* orbiter
1996 *SOHO* orbiter
1997 *ACE* orbiter
2001 *GENESIS* orbiter
2006 *STEREO* orbiter
2018 *PARKER SOLAR PROBE*
         orbiter

MERCURY

1 x FLYBYS
1 x ORBITER

NOTABLE SPACECRAFT

1974 *MARINER 10* flyby
2011 *MESSENGER* orbiter

VENUS

18 x FLYBYS
8 x ORBITERS
6 x ENTRY PROBES
10 x LANDERS

NOTABLE SPACECRAFT

1961 *VENERA 1* flyby
1962 *MARINER 2* flyby
1967 *VENERA 4* entry probe
1974 *MARINER 10* flyby
1975 *VENERA 9* lander
1982 *VENERA 13* lander
1990 *MAGELLAN* orbiter

THE MOON

22 x FLYBYS
30 x ORBITERS
3 x SAMPLE RETURNS
7 x IMPACTORS
10 x LANDERS   4 x ROVERS
6 x MANNED MISSIONS

NOTABLE SPACECRAFT

1959 *LUNA 1* probe
1966 *LUNA 9* lander
1969 *APOLLO 11* manned lander
1970 *LUNOKHOD 1* rover
2008 *CHANDRAYAAN 1* impactor
2018 *YUTU-2* rover

MARS

9 x FLYBYS
14 x ORBITERS
6 x LANDERS
4 x ROVERS

NOTABLE SPACECRAFT

1964 *MARINER 4* orbiter
1971 *MARINER 9* orbiter
1975 *VIKING 1* lander
1997 *SOJOURNER* rover
2004 *OPPORTUNITY* rover
2005 *MRO* orbiter
2011 *CURIOSITY* rover
2018 *INSIGHT* lander

ASTEROIDS

11 x FLYBYS
3 x ORBITERS
3 x SAMPLE RETURNS
2 x LANDERS

NOTABLE SPACECRAFT

1991 *GALILEO* flyby (GASPRA)
2000 *NEAR* orbiter/lander (EROS)
2005 *HAYABUSA*
         sample return (ITOKAWA)
2011 *DAWN* orbiter (VESTA)
2018 *HAYABUSA 2*
         orbiter/lander (RYUGU)

SPACESHIP FIRSTS

LUNA 1 AND LUNA 3

Launched in 1959, the Soviet Union's *Luna 1* was the first probe to be sent into space. It was supposed to land on the Moon but missed its target and instead went into orbit around the Sun. Later that year *Luna 3* took the first ever photos of the far side of the Moon (see p41).

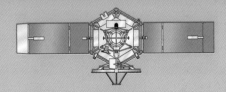

MARINER 2

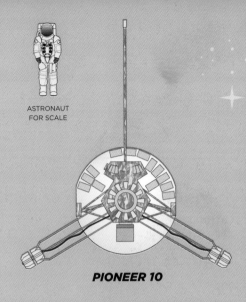

ASTRONAUT
FOR SCALE

PIONEER 10

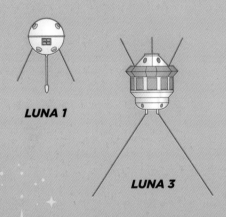

LUNA 1

LUNA 3

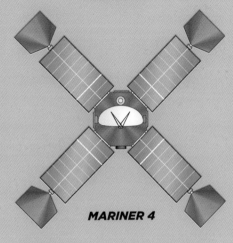

MARINER 4

MARINER 2 AND MARINER 4

In 1962, the American *Mariner 2* made the first successful flyby of Venus. In 1965, *Mariner 4* flew past Mars and beamed back photos of the planet – the first ever sent from deep space.

PIONEER 10 AND PIONEER 11

Launched in 1972 and 1973 respectively, *Pioneers 10* and *11* were the first probes to pass through the Asteroid Belt to record data about Jupiter. Today, *Pioneer 10* is continuing its journey into interstellar space towards the red star Aldebaran. It will take more than 2 million years to reach it. It's no longer in touch with Earth.

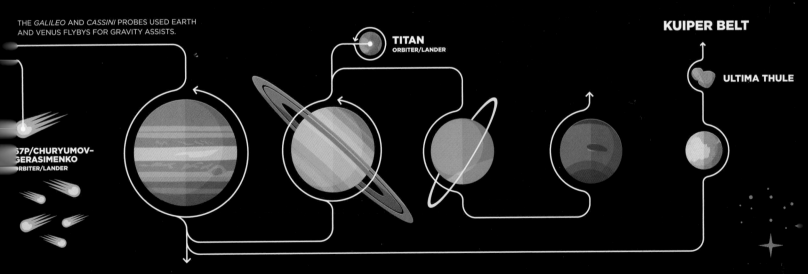

THE *GALILEO* AND *CASSINI* PROBES USED EARTH
AND VENUS FLYBYS FOR GRAVITY ASSISTS.

KUIPER BELT

TITAN
ORBITER/LANDER

ULTIMA THULE

67P/CHURYUMOV-
GERASIMENKO
ORBITER/LANDER

COMETS

3 x FLYBYS
x ORBITER
x SAMPLE RETURN
x IMPACTOR
x LANDER

NOTABLE SPACECRAFT
986 *GIOTTO* flyby (1P/HALLEY)
2005 *DEEP IMPACT* flyby/impactor
(9P/TEMPEL)
004 *STARDUST* sample return
(81P/WILD)
2014 *PHILAE* lander
(67P/CHURYUMOV-GERASIMENKO)

JUPITER

8 x FLYBYS
2 x ORBITERS
1 x ENTRY PROBE

SPACECRAFT
1973 *PIONEER 10* flyby
1974 *PIONEER 11* flyby
1979 *VOYAGER 1 & 2* flyby
1992 *ULYSSES* flyby
1995 *GALILEO* orbiter/probe
2000 *CASSINI-HUYGENS* flyby
2007 *NEW HORIZONS* flyby
2016 *JUNO* orbiter

SATURN

3 x FLYBYS
1 x ORBITER
1 x LANDER

SPACECRAFT
1979 *PIONEER 11* flyby
1980 *VOYAGER 1* flyby
1981 *VOYAGER 2* flyby
2004 *CASSINI* orbiter
2005 *HUYGENS* lander (TITAN)

URANUS

1 x FLYBY

SPACECRAFT
1986 *VOYAGER 2* flyby

NEPTUNE

1 x FLYBY

SPACECRAFT
1989 *VOYAGER 2* flyby

PLUTO

1 x FLYBY

SPACECRAFT
2015 *NEW HORIZONS* flyby

SIZE AND DISTANCE NOT TO SCALE

MERCURY

Small and speedy, Mercury is the planet that lies closest to the Sun. Travelling in a squashed, elliptical orbit, Mercury is only 46 million km (28 million miles) from the Sun at its closest point and 70 million km (43 million miles) at its furthest.

MARINER 10

For decades, the only close-up view we had of Mercury came from the *Mariner 10* probe – the first spacecraft to slingshot itself around another planet. *Mariner 10* used Venus' gravity to slow it down and change its flight path, before it passed Mercury in 1974. Fitted with a shield to protect against the Sun's rays, *Mariner 10* passed 320km (200 miles) above Mercury, taking photos and mapping the surface as it went. The photos showed a cratered world that had been bombarded by rocks.

⬆ ARTIST'S IMPRESSION OF *MESSENGER* IN ORBIT AROUND MERCURY.

MESSENGER

Mariner 10 had given humans their first glimpse of the Solar System's smallest planet. But it would be another 30 years before NASA launched a follow-up spacecraft, *Messenger*, to study the planet in more detail. To get to Mercury from Earth, *Messenger* had to journey across 7.9 million km (4.9 million miles) of space over nearly seven years. *Messenger* orbited Mercury until 2015, discovering, among other things, evidence of water ice at its poles.

BEPICOLOMBO

The *Mariner 10* and *Messenger* missions showed Mercury to be a mysterious place. One puzzle was its high levels of potassium and sulphur. To find out more about the planet's origin, the European Space Agency and Japanese *BepiColombo* mission was launched in 2018. *BepiColombo* is scheduled to enter Mercury's orbit in 2025.

TWO THIRDS OF MERCURY'S MASS IS MADE UP OF ITS **IRON CORE**, WHICH IS UNUSUALLY THICK FOR A ROCKY PLANET.

◉ COLOUR IMAGE CONSTRUCTED FROM OBSERVATIONS MADE BY *MESSENGER* IN FEBRUARY 2013.

◉ PLANET SHOWN WITHOUT COLOUR EFFECTS ADDED.

MERCURY

FROM EARTH, MERCURY CAN SOMETIMES BE SEEN **PASSING ACROSS THE FACE OF THE SUN**, AS IN THIS IMAGE.

MERCURY IS ONLY **TILTED** TWO DEGREES ON ITS **AXIS**, WHICH MEANS THERE ARE **NO SEASONS** ON THE PLANET.

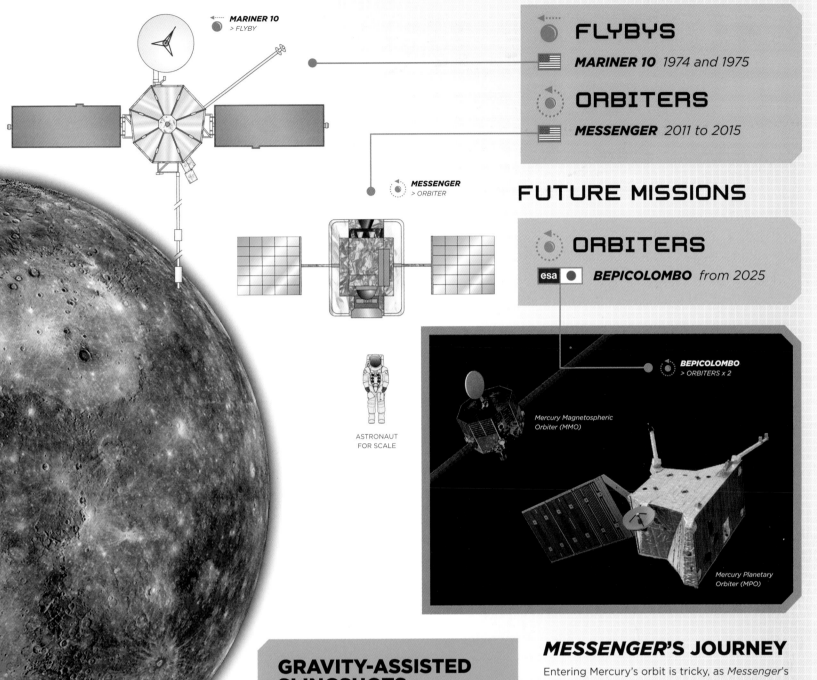

←--- ● **FLYBYS**

🇺🇸 **MARINER 10** *1974 and 1975*

◁·· ◉ **ORBITERS**

🇺🇸 **MESSENGER** *2011 to 2015*

←--- **MARINER 10**
● > *FLYBY*

··◉ **MESSENGER**
> *ORBITER*

FUTURE MISSIONS

◉ **ORBITERS**

esa ● **BEPICOLOMBO** *from 2025*

··◉ **BEPICOLOMBO**
> *ORBITERS x 2*

Mercury Magnetospheric
Orbiter (MMO)

Mercury Planetary
Orbiter (MPO)

ASTRONAUT
FOR SCALE

GRAVITY-ASSISTED SLINGSHOTS

For long-distance missions to faraway worlds, a gravity assist, or slingshot technique, is used. Simply, this involves a spacecraft using the gravitational field of a planet en route to its target to change its speed and sometimes its path.

MESSENGER'S JOURNEY

Entering Mercury's orbit is tricky, as *Messenger*'s journey there demonstrates. Flying towards Mercury means flying towards the Sun, which speeds a spacecraft up. Unless a spacecraft can brake when it gets to Mercury, it will fly straight into the Sun. To slow down, gravity-assisted slingshots around other planets are needed.

TIMELINE OF *MESSENGER*'S ROUTE:

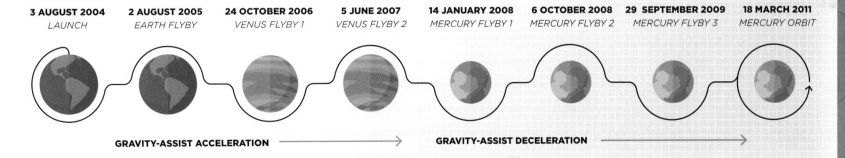

3 AUGUST 2004	**2 AUGUST 2005**	**24 OCTOBER 2006**	**5 JUNE 2007**	**14 JANUARY 2008**	**6 OCTOBER 2008**	**29 SEPTEMBER 2009**	**18 MARCH 2011**
LAUNCH	*EARTH FLYBY*	*VENUS FLYBY 1*	*VENUS FLYBY 2*	*MERCURY FLYBY 1*	*MERCURY FLYBY 2*	*MERCURY FLYBY 3*	*MERCURY ORBIT*

GRAVITY-ASSIST ACCELERATION →

GRAVITY-ASSIST DECELERATION →

THE TRAVELLER'S GUIDE TO MERCURY

Mercury is a tiny, tortured world with a pockmarked surface and no protective atmosphere. However, Mercury's front-row view of the Sun – where it appears three times bigger than on Earth – is spectacular. Don't forget a pair of sunglasses or two!

LANDING

The trick to landing on Mercury is to take it slowly. Spacecraft taking the direct route are pulled into the Sun's orbit and get faster as they get closer – too fast to stop. You'll need to slingshot around other planets to change direction, but slowing down means it will take months to get there – bring books for the journey! Take a sky crane to ease your lander's descent to the surface.

KIT BOX

- ✓ **LANDER WITH A SKY CRANE**
- ✓ **SPACESUIT WITH RADIATION PROTECTION**
- ✓ **ICE-MINING EQUIPMENT**
- ✓ **SUNGLASSES**

Take care on your descent to the craggy surface.

SURFACE

With no atmosphere, Mercury is not protected against objects striking it from space. The surface has a crater-marked landscape, a bit like our Moon's. Keep an eye out for meteorites while you're there! Your lander will need an oxygen supply and some serious heat-shielding. If you land on the side of the planet facing the Sun, expect temperatures to rocket up to a sweltering 430°C (806°F)! If you land in darkness, the opposite problem applies – the temperature can plummet to -180°C (-292°F). Good heating and cooling systems on your lander are a must.

EXPLORING

Remember to wear a spacesuit with extra radiation protection against solar rays. The gravity on Mercury is only 38% of that on Earth, so you'll be able to move in triple-quick time. Head to one of the poles – there is evidence of water ice in Mercury's polar craters, so take mining equipment. The ice can be split into two chemical elements – oxygen and hydrogen, so you'll be able to breathe and have rocket propellant to get home. You did think about fuel to get home, didn't you?

Mercury is the closest planet to the Sun, which will appear vast in the sky.

MERCURY DATA FILE

average **58 million km** (36 million miles) *from the Sun.*

THE SUN

MERCURY · VENUS · EARTH · MARS · JUPITER · SATURN · URANUS · NEPTUNE

SIZE AND DISTANCE NOT TO SCALE

TEMPERATURE

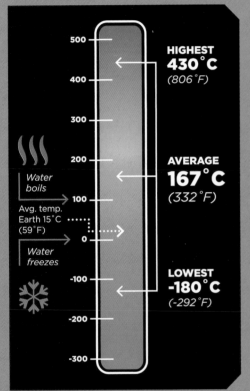

- 500
- 400
- 300
- 200
- 100
- 0
- -100
- -200
- -300

HIGHEST 430°C (806°F)

AVERAGE 167°C (332°F)

LOWEST -180°C (-292°F)

Water boils

Avg. temp. Earth 15°C (59°F)

Water freezes

SIZE

MERCURY

THE MOON · EARTH

AVERAGE DIAMETER

4879km
(3032 miles)

Mercury is about two-fifths the diameter of Earth and slightly wider than our Moon.

MOONS: 0

AVERAGE SPEED

47km/sec
(29 miles/sec)

Mercury travels through space at 47km/sec, faster than any other planet in the Solar System.

EARTH: 30km/sec (18.5 miles/sec)

CALENDAR

Length of a day
58.6 Earth days

Length of a year
88 Earth days

SURFACE CHARACTER

EXOSPHERE:

Although it does not have an atmosphere like Earth's, Mercury has a thin, outer atmosphere called an exosphere. This contains low levels of oxygen, sodium, hydrogen and potassium, and was created from atoms blasted off Mercury's surface by meteorites and solar winds.

GRAVITY:

x 0.38
of EARTH

If you weigh 70kg (11st) on Earth, you will weigh 27kg (4st) on Mercury.

O_2 OXYGEN
42%

Na SODIUM
29%

H_2 HYDROGEN
22%

OTHER GASES
7%

SPOTLIGHT

CALORIS CRATER

Around 4 billion years ago, a 100km-wide (60 mile) asteroid struck Mercury. Landing with the impact of a 1 trillion-megaton bomb, the asteroid left a 1550km-wide (963 mile) crater, today known as Caloris (shown below).

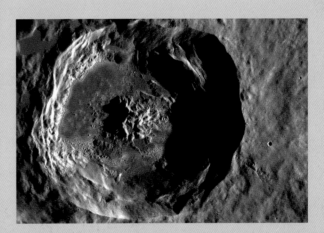

VENUS

For centuries, the secrets of Venus' surface lay shrouded in mystery. The brightest planet in our night sky is covered by a thick blanket of cloud. Did a world brimming with life lie beneath?

FLYBYS

In the 19th century, some scientists imagined a world that mirrored Earth. The Soviet Union launched the first flyby of Venus in 1961. Its *Venera 1* spacecraft passed within 100,000km (62,000 miles) of the planet, but then lost contact. In 1962, the US *Mariner 2* came as close as 35,000km (21,700 miles) to Venus. The spacecraft, however, beamed back some unsettling data – Venus had a surface temperature of nearly 500°C (932°F). Another US flyby, *Mariner 10*, reported hurricane-force winds.

LANDERS

The Soviet Union's *Venera 4* was the first to enter Venus' thick atmosphere, which it reported to be mainly carbon dioxide, before it melted. In 1975, *Venera 9* parachuted to Venus' surface and took the first ever photos, before failing 53 minutes later. The photos and data revealed why: Venus was a vision of hell. The planet has a rocky, desolate surface, where the temperature is 475°C (887°F) and the toxic atmosphere a crushing 92 times higher in pressure than on Earth.

THE *MAGELLAN* ORBITER IS DEPLOYED FROM THE SPACE SHUTTLE *ATLANTIS* HIGH ABOVE EARTH IN 1989 BEFORE HEADING TO VENUS.

ORBITERS

In 1989, the US *Magellan* became the first orbiter to be launched from a Space Shuttle. It mapped the entire surface of Venus, showing 85% of it is covered with lava flows. This indicates high volcanic activity in the past. Without water to erode them, the lava flows could be hundreds of millions of years old. Further back in time, Venus was probably covered with oceans. Learning what turned it into such an inhospitable world is key to understanding the prospects for life on other rocky planets.

VENUS' THICK **SULPHURIC CLOUDS** MAKE IT IMPOSSIBLE TO VIEW THE SURFACE THROUGH AN OPTICAL TELESCOPE.

A FALSE-COLOUR RADAR VIEW OF VENUS TAKEN THROUGH THE CLOUDS CAPTURED BY THE *MAGELLAN* PROBE IN 1991.

A VIEW OF VENUS CAPTURED BY THE *MARINER 10* PROBE ON 5 FEBRUARY 1974 SHOWING ITS DENSE LAYERS OF CLOUDS.

OF THE 11 SOVIET PROBES SENT TO VENUS, NONE HAS SURVIVED LONGER THAN **TWO HOURS** ON THE SURFACE.

3-D PERSPECTIVE VIEW OF MAAT MONS, THE HIGHEST VOLCANO ON VENUS.

VENUS IS THE **BRIGHTEST PLANET** IN OUR NIGHT SKY. ONLY THE MOON IS BRIGHTER.

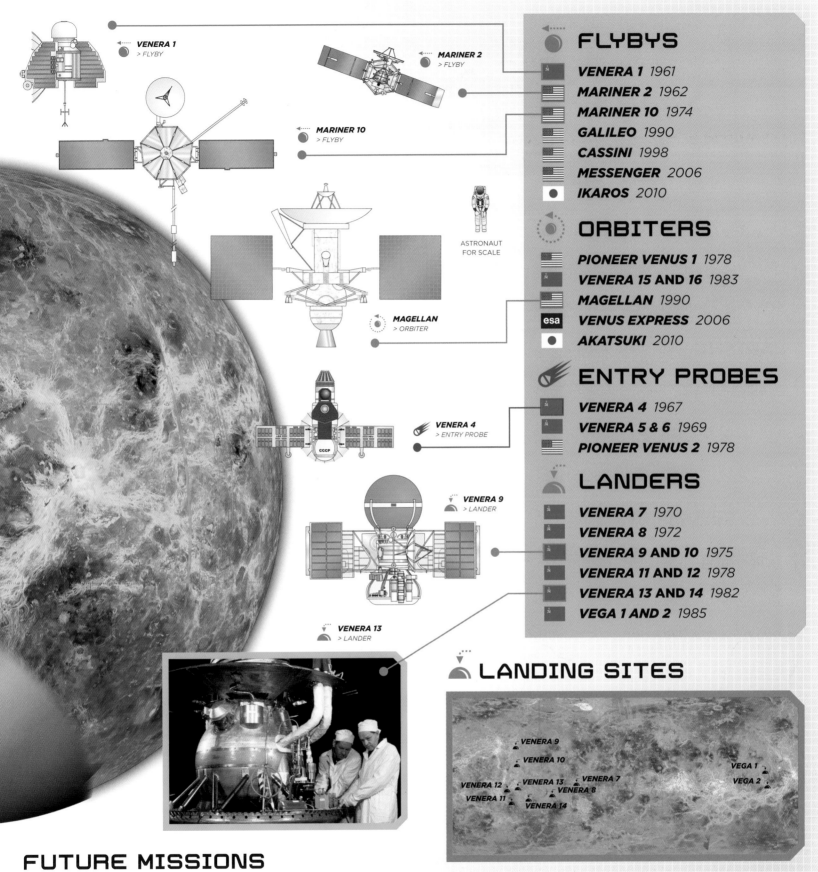

VENERA 1
> FLYBY

MARINER 2
> FLYBY

MARINER 10
> FLYBY

ASTRONAUT
FOR SCALE

MAGELLAN
> ORBITER

VENERA 4
> ENTRY PROBE

VENERA 9
> LANDER

VENERA 13
> LANDER

FLYBYS

VENERA 1 *1961*
MARINER 2 *1962*
MARINER 10 *1974*
GALILEO *1990*
CASSINI *1998*
MESSENGER *2006*
IKAROS *2010*

ORBITERS

PIONEER VENUS 1 *1978*
VENERA 15 AND 16 *1983*
MAGELLAN *1990*
VENUS EXPRESS *2006*
AKATSUKI *2010*

ENTRY PROBES

VENERA 4 *1967*
VENERA 5 & 6 *1969*
PIONEER VENUS 2 *1978*

LANDERS

VENERA 7 *1970*
VENERA 8 *1972*
VENERA 9 AND 10 *1975*
VENERA 11 AND 12 *1978*
VENERA 13 AND 14 *1982*
VEGA 1 AND 2 *1985*

LANDING SITES

VENERA 9
VENERA 10
VENERA 12   VENERA 13   VENERA 7   VEGA 1
VENERA 11   VENERA 8   VEGA 2
              VENERA 14

FUTURE MISSIONS

ORBITER India's *Orbiter* is planned to visit Venus in 2023 to study its atmosphere.

VERITAS Planned for the mid-2020s, the US *Veritas* orbiter will use high-resolution radar to study Venus' topography (its physical features).

DAVINCI Scheduled for launch in the mid-2020s, the US *Davinci* spacecraft will launch a lander to photograph Venus' surface.

LLISSE The most ambitious Venus mission, the US's *Long-Lived In-Situ Solar System Explorer* (*LLISSE*) will stay on Venus' surface for several months collecting atmospheric data.

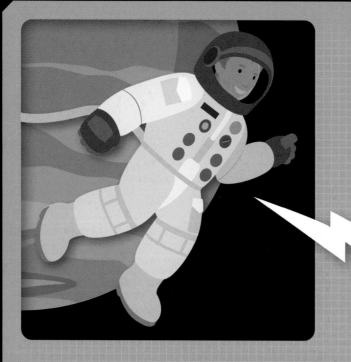

THE TRAVELLER'S GUIDE TO VENUS

No humans have ever been to Venus. Why not? Venus is a fiendishly hot planet, whipped by hurricane-force winds in its upper atmosphere with much higher pressure than on Earth. Don't let this put you off, however. A manned trip to Venus could be possible with the right gear.

LANDING

Pressure on Venus is so intense that any normal spacecraft would be crushed in minutes. The atmospheric pressure is equivalent to diving to a depth of around 1km (3,300ft). However, the deepest part of the ocean on Earth, the Mariana Trench, is nearly 11km (36,300ft). Five deep-sea craft have withstood a descent to this depth, so it is possible to build a craft that could hold out. The intense heat is the next problem...

KIT BOX

✓ **LANDER/ROVER**

✓ **ENOUGH OXYGEN FOR THE STAY**

✓ **REFRIGERATED FOOD AND DRINK**

✓ **AIRSHIP**

Artist's impression of what awaits you on Venus.

SURFACE

Travellers to Venus won't need to pack a jumper. The planet's surface is one of the hottest places in our Solar System, with temperatures of around 465°C (870°F). Visitors to Venus have to think carefully about their lander design and would need to develop some kind of advanced air conditioner. The system would need to use a different fluid to those used on Earth. Hydrogen or helium are possibilities, but a specially made liquid is most likely – it would need to have a boiling point similar to Venus' surface temperature.

EXPLORING

It's probably not a good idea to try to set foot on the planet. But Venus' upper atmosphere is around 20% oxygen and 70 % nitrogen, making it similar to that on Earth. Missions to stay in Venus' orbit have been suggested, including living on 50km-high (30 mile) mountains built by robot bulldozers or living in a cloud city or a giant airship that orbits the planet.

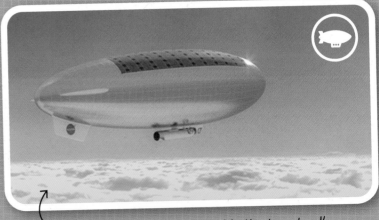

NASA once planned to use a craft like this to explore Venus.

➤ VENUS DATA FILE

THE SUN

average **108 million km** (67 million miles) *from the Sun.*

MERCURY · **VENUS** · EARTH · MARS · JUPITER · SATURN · URANUS · NEPTUNE

SIZE AND DISTANCE NOT TO SCALE

➤ TEMPERATURE

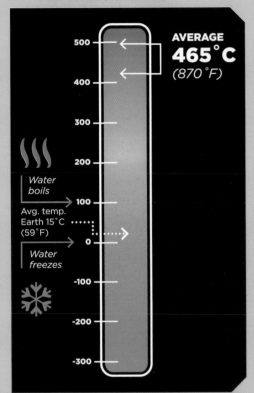

500
400
300
200
100
0
-100
-200
-300

**AVERAGE
465°C**
(870°F)

Water boils
Avg. temp.
Earth 15°C
(59°F)
Water freezes

➤ SIZE

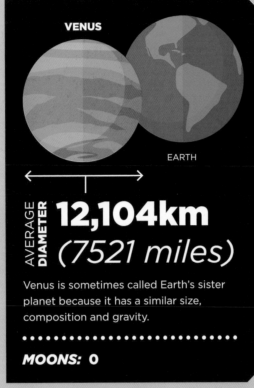

VENUS

EARTH

AVERAGE DIAMETER
12,104km
(7521 miles)

Venus is sometimes called Earth's sister planet because it has a similar size, composition and gravity.

MOONS: 0

➤ AVERAGE SPEED

35km/sec
(22 miles/sec)

Venus is the second-fastest planet in the Solar System – it whizzes through space at 35km/sec.

EARTH: 30km/sec (18.5 miles/sec)

➤ CALENDAR

Length of a day
243 Earth days

Length of a year
225 Earth days

➤ SURFACE CHARACTER

ATMOSPHERE:

The high levels of carbon dioxide trap heat close to the planet's surface. This makes Venus the hottest planet in the Solar System, with an extremely inhospitable atmosphere. This overcast outlook is frequently broken up by lightning.

GRAVITY:

x 0.91
of EARTH

If you weigh 70kg (11st) on Earth, you will weigh 64kg (10st) on Venus.

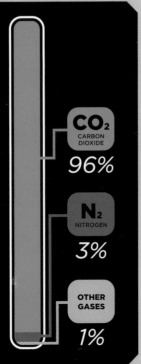

CO₂
CARBON DIOXIDE
96%

N₂
NITROGEN
3%

OTHER GASES
1%

➤ SPOTLIGHT

SPINNING AROUND

Venus and Uranus are the only planets that have a retrograde action. This means they spin in the opposite direction to all other planets in our Solar System. It has been suggested that at some point, many, many years ago, Venus collided with something that reversed its direction. It also spins so slowly that it's the only planet with a day that is longer than its year!

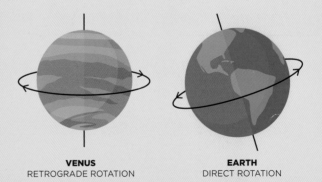

VENUS
RETROGRADE ROTATION

EARTH
DIRECT ROTATION

MARS

Mars is a barren world with no visible life. And yet, for millions of years, vast lakes covered its surface and deep rivers ran through valleys of rock. Could life have existed there? We have sent more spacecraft to Mars than any other planet to try to unlock its mysteries.

ORBITERS

Some people were hoping to see alien civilisations on Mars when the *Mariner 4* probe first photographed it during a 1965 flyby. Closer images taken by the 1971 orbiter *Mariner 9* confirmed there were no aliens, but the planet is so complex and fascinating that we kept sending more spacecraft. Today a fleet of Martian orbiters continues its studies. The orbiters are partly managed by the *Mars Reconnaissance Orbiter (MRO)*, which can photograph an object as small as a tennis ball on the surface.

LANDERS

In 1975, *Viking 1* and *2* orbited Mars and dropped landers onto its surface. Photos revealed a rocky, rusty-red landscape under a pink sky, but their tests for organic material in the soil were inconclusive. Another 14 landers have since been launched. Some of them crash-landed or experienced equipment failure. A recent success was the 2018 *InSight* lander, which is probing the planet's surface. This may reveal answers about the formation of the Solar System's four rocky planets (Mercury, Venus, Earth and Mars).

⊕ AN ARTIST'S IMPRESSION OF THE *INSIGHT* LANDER PROBING THE SURFACE OF MARS.

ROVERS

In 1997, the *Mars Pathfinder* delivered a rover to explore the surface of Mars. Equipped with solar panels, the *Sojourner* rover sent back images of eroded gullies, which indicated there had been flowing water in the past. Two larger rovers, *Spirit* and *Opportunity*, able to tackle virtually any terrain, were dispatched in 2003 and landed on opposite sides of the planet. The *Opportunity* rover explored Mars for 14 years, but finally stopped communicating after being caught in a dust storm in 2018.

IT WOULD TAKE A TEAM OF ASTRONAUTS OVER **TWO YEARS** TO TRAVEL TO MARS AND BACK.

THE BRIGHT POLAR CAPS ON MARS ARE VISIBLE FROM TELESCOPES ON EARTH AND ARE MADE OF WATER ICE AND FROZEN CARBON DIOXIDE.

◉ GLOBAL COLOUR IMAGE CAPTURED BY THE ORBITER *VIKING 1* IN 1976.

THE **LAUNCH WINDOW**, WHEN MARS IS AT ITS CLOSEST, IS ONCE EVERY **26 MONTHS**.

SCIENTISTS BELIEVE MARS ONCE HAD AN **OCEAN** CONTAINING MORE **WATER** THAN THE **ARCTIC OCEAN** ON EARTH.

VALLES MARINERIS IS THE LARGEST CANYON IN THE SOLAR SYSTEM.

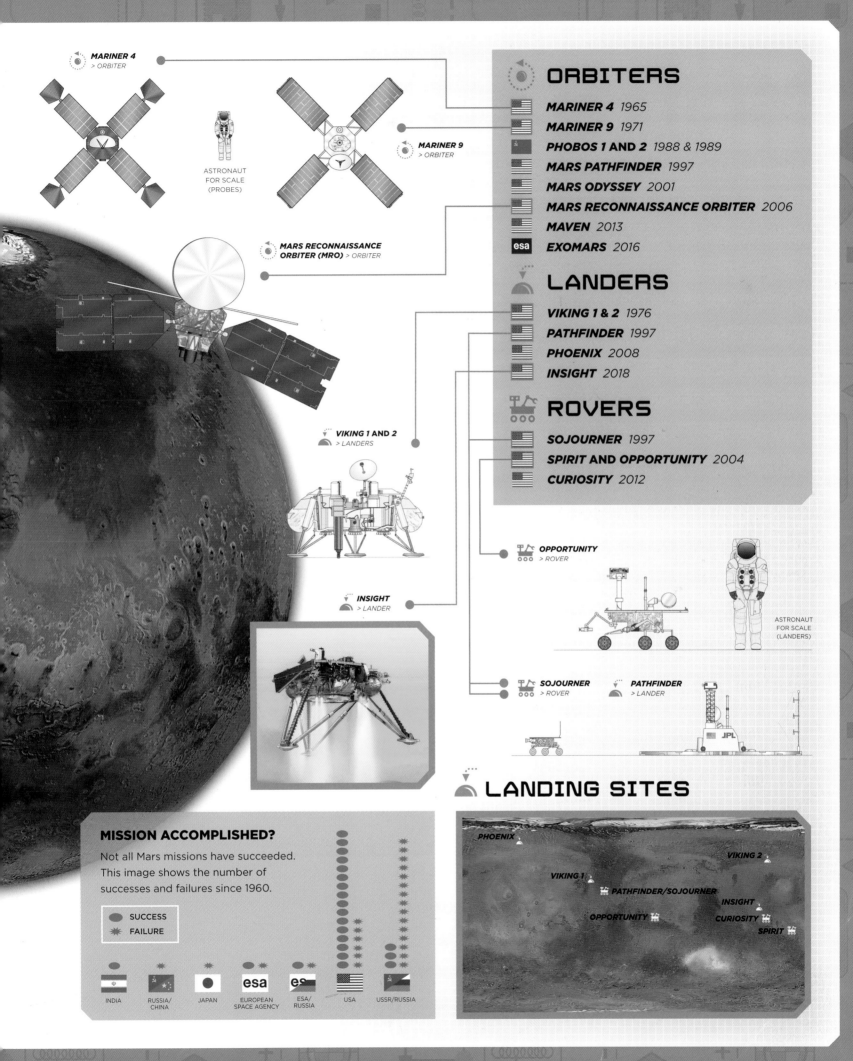

MARINER 4
> ORBITER

MARINER 9
> ORBITER

ASTRONAUT
FOR SCALE
(PROBES)

MARS RECONNAISSANCE
ORBITER (MRO) > ORBITER

ORBITERS

MARINER 4 *1965*
MARINER 9 *1971*
PHOBOS 1 AND 2 *1988 & 1989*
MARS PATHFINDER *1997*
MARS ODYSSEY *2001*
MARS RECONNAISSANCE ORBITER *2006*
MAVEN *2013*
EXOMARS *2016*

LANDERS

VIKING 1 & 2 *1976*
PATHFINDER *1997*
PHOENIX *2008*
INSIGHT *2018*

ROVERS

SOJOURNER *1997*
SPIRIT AND OPPORTUNITY *2004*
CURIOSITY *2012*

VIKING 1 AND 2
> LANDERS

INSIGHT
> LANDER

OPPORTUNITY
> ROVER

ASTRONAUT
FOR SCALE
(LANDERS)

SOJOURNER
> ROVER

PATHFINDER
> LANDER

JPL

LANDING SITES

MISSION ACCOMPLISHED?

Not all Mars missions have succeeded.
This image shows the number of
successes and failures since 1960.

● SUCCESS
✳ FAILURE

INDIA

RUSSIA/
CHINA

JAPAN

EUROPEAN
SPACE AGENCY

ESA/
RUSSIA

USA

USSR/RUSSIA

PHOENIX

VIKING 2

VIKING 1

PATHFINDER/SOJOURNER

INSIGHT

OPPORTUNITY

CURIOSITY

SPIRIT

MARS ROVERS

A robotic, car-sized laboratory on wheels, the *Curiosity* rover
was sent to Mars to explore a 150km-wide (90mile) crater,
which once contained water. The primary aim was to search
for organic material. Expected to end in 2014, *Curiosity*'s
two-year mission has been extended indefinitely.

CURIOSITY ROVER

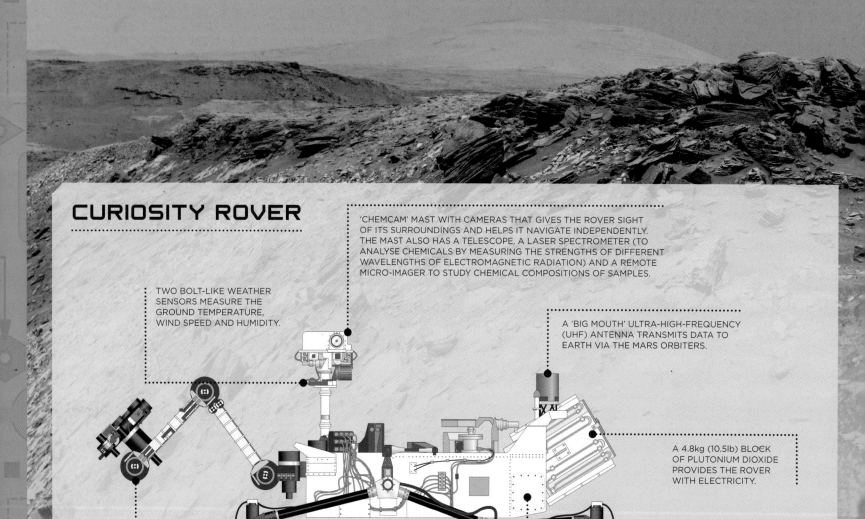

'CHEMCAM' MAST WITH CAMERAS THAT GIVES THE ROVER SIGHT
OF ITS SURROUNDINGS AND HELPS IT NAVIGATE INDEPENDENTLY.
THE MAST ALSO HAS A TELESCOPE, A LASER SPECTROMETER (TO
ANALYSE CHEMICALS BY MEASURING THE STRENGTHS OF DIFFERENT
WAVELENGTHS OF ELECTROMAGNETIC RADIATION) AND A REMOTE
MICRO-IMAGER TO STUDY CHEMICAL COMPOSITIONS OF SAMPLES.

TWO BOLT-LIKE WEATHER
SENSORS MEASURE THE
GROUND TEMPERATURE,
WIND SPEED AND HUMIDITY.

A 'BIG MOUTH' ULTRA-HIGH-FREQUENCY
(UHF) ANTENNA TRANSMITS DATA TO
EARTH VIA THE MARS ORBITERS.

A 4.8kg (10.5lb) BLOCK
OF PLUTONIUM DIOXIDE
PROVIDES THE ROVER
WITH ELECTRICITY.

A 2.1m LONG (6.5ft), MULTI-JOINTED
ROBOTIC ARM WITH A 'HAND' AT THE
END SCOOPS UP MARTIAN SOIL TO
ANALYSE ITS CHEMICAL COMPOUNDS.
ALSO FEATURES A DRILL FOR
COLLECTING SAMPLES.

SIX 50cm (20in)
DIAMETER ALUMINIUM
WHEELS, WITH
TITANIUM SPRINGS
FOR SUSPENSION.

WATER-FINDING SENSOR THAT CAN DETECT
HYDROGEN 1m   (3.2ft) BELOW THE
SURFACE
AND MINUTE TRACES OF WATER IN THE GROUND.

LENGTH:
5.1m (16.7ft)

HEIGHT:
2.2m (7.2ft)

WHEELS (DIAMETER):
50.8cm (20in)

WEIGHT:
8.99kg (19.8lb)

TOP SPEED:
5cm/sec (23in/sec)

SELF-PORTRAIT OF
NASA'S *CURIOSITY*
ROVER TAKEN ON MARS
ON 5 AUGUST 2015.

DISTANCES DRIVEN ON OTHER WORLDS

SOJOURNER 1997
0.1km (0.06 miles)

MARS

MOON

SPIRIT 2004–2010
7.7km (4.8 miles)

CURIOSITY 2012–PRESENT (AS OF 1 JANUARY 2020)
21.6km (13.4 miles)

OPPORTUNITY 2003–2018
45.2km (28.1 miles)

LUNOKHOD 2 1973
39km (24.2 miles)

APOLLO 17 LUNAR ROVER 1972
35.7km (22.2 miles)

LANDING ON MARS

The landing of the *Curiosity* rover on Mars was an ambitious sequence of complex engineering and daring that its designers referred to as 'seven minutes of hell'. It required the USD$2.5 billion rover to touch down gently enough so as not to damage its fragile scientific equipment.

Curiosity was travelling at 10 times the speed of a bullet when it entered the atmosphere of Mars, and it had to lose a lot of this speed quickly or it would crash onto the surface. The atmosphere of Mars is thick enough to cause a fast-moving object to heat up rapidly, which is another reason to slow down. On Earth, returning spacecraft use parachutes to slow down, but the atmosphere of Mars is too thin for parachutes to work properly. For *Curiosity*, the solution was a sky crane. This is how the landing sequence worked.

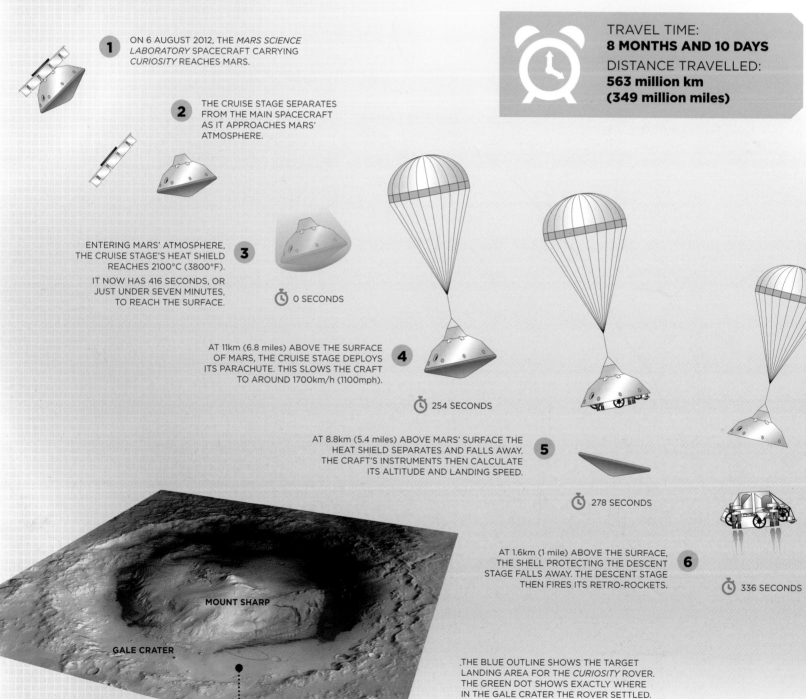

1 ON 6 AUGUST 2012, THE *MARS SCIENCE LABORATORY* SPACECRAFT CARRYING *CURIOSITY* REACHES MARS.

2 THE CRUISE STAGE SEPARATES FROM THE MAIN SPACECRAFT AS IT APPROACHES MARS' ATMOSPHERE.

3 ENTERING MARS' ATMOSPHERE, THE CRUISE STAGE'S HEAT SHIELD REACHES 2100°C (3800°F).

IT NOW HAS 416 SECONDS, OR JUST UNDER SEVEN MINUTES, TO REACH THE SURFACE.

0 SECONDS

4 AT 11km (6.8 miles) ABOVE THE SURFACE OF MARS, THE CRUISE STAGE DEPLOYS ITS PARACHUTE. THIS SLOWS THE CRAFT TO AROUND 1700km/h (1100mph).

254 SECONDS

5 AT 8.8km (5.4 miles) ABOVE MARS' SURFACE THE HEAT SHIELD SEPARATES AND FALLS AWAY. THE CRAFT'S INSTRUMENTS THEN CALCULATE ITS ALTITUDE AND LANDING SPEED.

278 SECONDS

6 AT 1.6km (1 mile) ABOVE THE SURFACE, THE SHELL PROTECTING THE DESCENT STAGE FALLS AWAY. THE DESCENT STAGE THEN FIRES ITS RETRO-ROCKETS.

336 SECONDS

TRAVEL TIME:
8 MONTHS AND 10 DAYS
DISTANCE TRAVELLED:
**563 million km
(349 million miles)**

MOUNT SHARP

GALE CRATER

THE BLUE OUTLINE SHOWS THE TARGET LANDING AREA FOR THE *CURIOSITY* ROVER. THE GREEN DOT SHOWS EXACTLY WHERE IN THE GALE CRATER THE ROVER SETTLED.

EARLIER EXPLORERS

OPPORTUNITY LANDING SEQUENCE

OPPORTUNITY ROVER

1

2

Nine years before *Curiosity* set off for Mars, *Spirit* and *Opportunity* were sent to scope out the planet. The sky crane hadn't yet been developed, so they had bumpier landings surrounded by airbags. Their missions were originally only meant to last 90 days each, but both rovers simply kept going! *Spirit* lasted until 2010, but *Opportunity* kept trundling around Mars until 2018 when a huge dust storm finally cut off all communication.

1 THE LANDER IS PROTECTED BY LARGE AIRBAGS AFTER FALLING AWAY FROM ITS PARACHUTE.

2 THE *OPPORTUNITY* ROVER EMERGES FROM INSIDE THE PROTECTIVE AIRBAGS.

GETTING THE *CURIOSITY* ROVER TO MARS TOOK:

$2.5 BILLION : **250** SCIENTISTS : **160** ENGINEERS

7 WITH 19m (62ft) TO THE SURFACE, THE 7.5m (24ft) CABLES MAKING UP THE SKY CRANE LOWER THE ROVER DOWN FROM THE DESCENT STAGE.

8 AT 3.5m (11.4ft) ABOVE THE SURFACE, *CURIOSITY*'S WHEELS POP OUT FOR LANDING.

9 AFTER IT LOWERS *CURIOSITY* TO THE GROUND, THE SKY CRANE FIRES ITSELF AWAY SO IT WILL NOT LAND ON THE ROVER. LANDING COMPLETE!

400 SECONDS

416 SECONDS

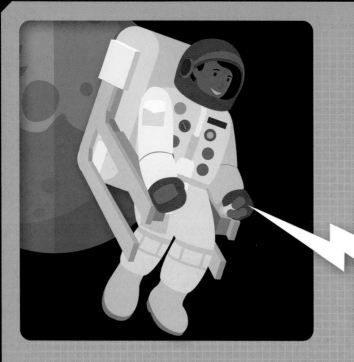

THE TRAVELLER'S GUIDE TO MARS

Plans to visit Mars have begun. Mars is a lot like Earth: it has seasons, a similar day length and water ice, but it is also an airless world with extreme temperatures. A quick jaunt to see the sights isn't on the cards – you'll need to make the fuel for the return journey during your stay!

LANDING

To survive even a short stint on Mars, you'll need tons of supplies, including oxygen, food and water. But landing such a heavy load on the Martian surface is no easy feat. It will require some sort of sky crane (see pages 62–63) to stop you from burning up in Mars' atmosphere, but also to slow you down enough to prevent a crash-landing. Humans can get bruised when touching down at 10 times the speed of a bullet!

KIT BOX

- ✓ **LONG-DISTANCE SPACECRAFT WITH A SKY CRANE**
- ✓ **SPACESUIT WITH EXTRA RADIATION PROOFING**
- ✓ **ENOUGH FOOD, OXYGEN AND WATER FOR THE STAY**
- ✓ **A HIGH-POWERED TORCH**

An aerial view of Olympus Mons.

SURFACE

The dusty, rusty-red surface of Mars is a long way from the scenic landscapes of Earth. You'll find it is not a particularly welcoming place for people. Temperatures on the Martian surface fluctuate from -140°C (-290°F) at night to 30°C (86°F) during the day. There is also no oxygen – the atmosphere is made of 95.3% carbon dioxide, which is unbreathable for humans. Both of these factors mean that you will need a spacesuit to survive on Mars – never take it off outdoors!

EXPLORING

Gravity on Mars is around 38% of that on Earth. You will feel lighter, be able to carry heavier loads and jump much longer distances, so you'll have no excuse not to climb one of Mars' must-see sights: Olympus Mons, the Solar System's highest volcano. At 22km (13 miles) high, it's nearly three times as high as Mount Everest, Earth's tallest mountain. Summer only occurs every 26 months, but its storms blow enough fine dust into the atmosphere to make it look like twilight for months on end. Bring a torch!

An artist's impression of settlers on Mars.

➤ MARS DATA FILE

average **228 million km** (142 million miles) *from the Sun.*

THE SUN

MERCURY   VENUS   EARTH   **MARS**   JUPITER   SATURN   URANUS   NEPTUNE

SIZE AND DISTANCE NOT TO SCALE

➤ TEMPERATURE

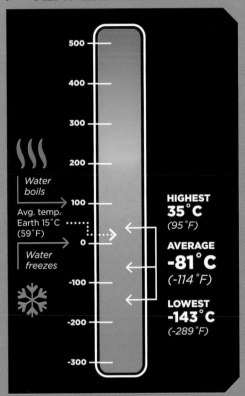

500
400
300
200
100
0
-100
-200
-300

Water boils

Avg. temp.
Earth 15°C
(59°F)

Water freezes

HIGHEST
35°C
(95°F)

AVERAGE
-81°C
(-114°F)

LOWEST
-143°C
(-289°F)

➤ SIZE

MARS

EARTH

AVERAGE DIAMETER

6791km
(4219 miles)

MOONS:
2

PHOBOS   DEIMOS

➤ AVERAGE SPEED

24km/sec
(15 miles/sec)

Mars orbits the Sun about 5km/sec slower than Earth – the further a planet is from the Sun, the slower it travels.

EARTH: 30km/sec (18.5 miles/sec)

➤ CALENDAR

Length of a day
24 hours, 37 minutes

Length of a year
687 days

➤ SURFACE CHARACTER

ATMOSPHERE:

Mars has a thinner atmosphere than Earth – 100 times thinner, in fact. The low gravitational pull allows more gases to escape into space. Although the maximum daytime temperatures can sound similar to Earth's, the lows are so much colder. Carbon dioxide snow – or 'dry ice' – sometimes falls.

GRAVITY:

x 0.38
of EARTH

If you weigh 70kg (11st) on Earth, you will weigh 27kg (4st) on Mars.

CO₂
CARBON DIOXIDE
95%

N₂
NITROGEN
3%

Ar
ARGON
1.5%

OTHER GASES
0.5%

➤ SPOTLIGHT

SNAKING STORMS

Towers of whirling dust stretching hundreds of metres wide whip across the Martian landscape. They can be up to 10 times the size of tornadoes on Earth and reduce visibility to zero.

JUPITER

Jupiter is by far the biggest planet in our Solar System, more than twice the size of all the other planets combined. Over 1,300 Earth-sized objects could fit inside this gas giant. Its outer stripes are clouds of ammonia, which drift across an atmosphere mainly composed of hydrogen and helium.

FLYBYS

In 1973, the *Pioneer 10* spacecraft passed through the Asteroid Belt to within 130,000km (80,000 miles) of Jupiter. From here, it sent back over 500 photos of the planet to Earth – the first close-ups we had ever seen of Jupiter. More flybys by *Pioneer 11*, *Voyager 1* and *2*, and *New Horizons* followed, each beaming back photos as they passed by on their grand tours of the Solar System. The pictures were a marvel, showing Jupiter to be like a mini Solar System all of its own, with at least 79 moons.

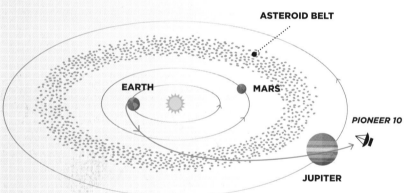

↑ *PIONEER 10*'S ROUTE THROUGH THE ASTEROID BELT TO JUPITER.

SYSTEM ORBITER

The flybys of Jupiter showed that the planet's radiation levels were low enough for spacecraft to enter its orbit. In 1989, the *Galileo* spacecraft was duly launched from Earth and arrived at the gas giant in 1995, spending two years touring Jupiter and its moons, before deliberately crashing a probe onto the planet. This sent back data for nearly an hour before imploding in the intense pressure and temperatures.

NEW ORBITER

In 2011, NASA launched its newest spacecraft to Jupiter: *Juno*. Arriving in 2016, *Juno* entered an elliptical orbit around Jupiter that took it from 8 million km (4.9 million miles) from the surface to just 4000km (2500 miles). From here, *Juno* has been collecting data about Jupiter's origin by using its high-tech instruments to measure its composition and gravitational fields. *Juno*'s cameras have sent back the best photos of Jupiter we have ever seen.

SOME SCIENTISTS ONCE THOUGHT JUPITER'S CORE WAS LIKE THICK, **BOILING MUD**. IT IS NOW BELIEVED TO BE A LARGE SOLID CORE.

◉ GLOBAL COLOUR IMAGE CAPTURED BY *VOYAGER 1* ON 27 FEBRUARY 1979.

JUPITER IS HOT: SCIENTISTS THINK THE PLANET IS AROUND **24,000°C (43,200°F)** AT ITS CORE.

↑ SPACECRAFT FLYING NEAR TO JUPITER HAVE CAPTURED IMAGES OF ITS RINGS, WHICH ARE MUCH FAINTER THAN THOSE AROUND SATURN.

ALL FOUR OUTER PLANETS HAVE RINGS. JUPITER'S **RING SYSTEM** IS FORMED FROM DUST CAUSED BY **METEOROIDS SMASHING** INTO ITS FOUR SMALL INNER MOONS.

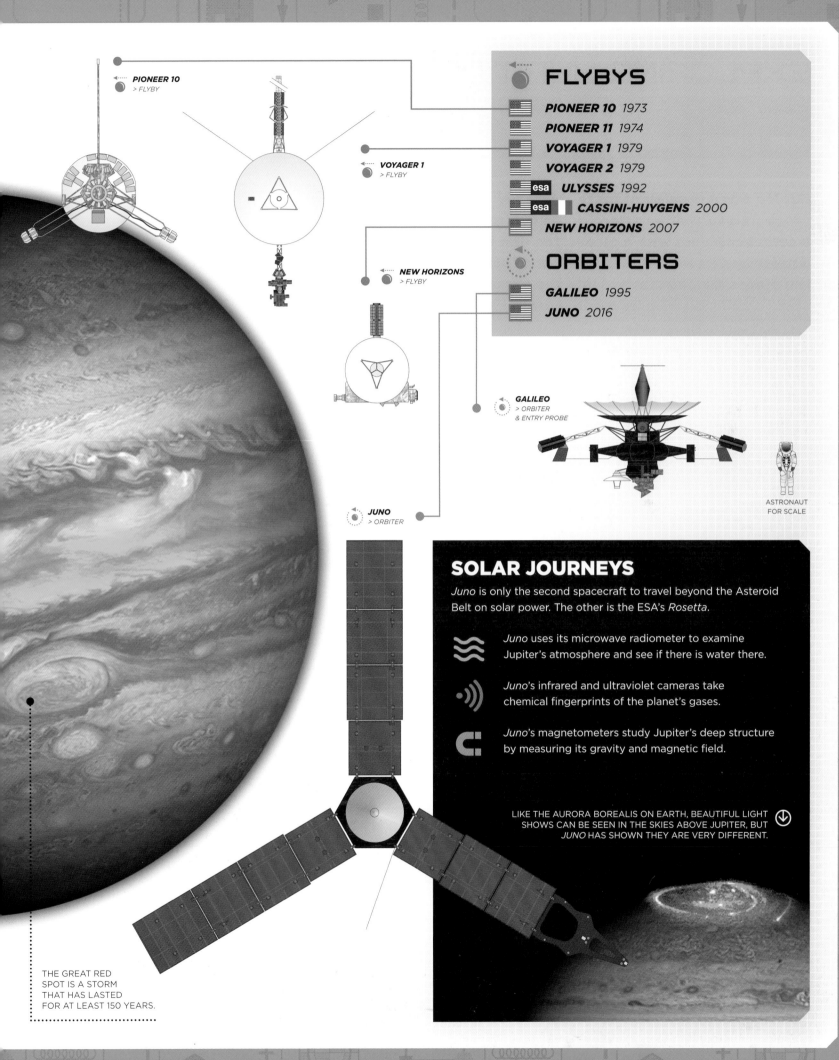

FLYBYS

🇺🇸	**PIONEER 10**	*1973*
🇺🇸	**PIONEER 11**	*1974*
🇺🇸	**VOYAGER 1**	*1979*
🇺🇸	**VOYAGER 2**	*1979*
🇺🇸 esa	**ULYSSES**	*1992*
🇺🇸 esa 🇮🇹	**CASSINI-HUYGENS**	*2000*
🇺🇸	**NEW HORIZONS**	*2007*

ORBITERS

🇺🇸	**GALILEO**	*1995*
🇺🇸	**JUNO**	*2016*

PIONEER 10
> FLYBY

VOYAGER 1
> FLYBY

NEW HORIZONS
> FLYBY

GALILEO
> ORBITER
& ENTRY PROBE

JUNO
> ORBITER

ASTRONAUT
FOR SCALE

SOLAR JOURNEYS

Juno is only the second spacecraft to travel beyond the Asteroid Belt on solar power. The other is the ESA's *Rosetta*.

Juno uses its microwave radiometer to examine Jupiter's atmosphere and see if there is water there.

Juno's infrared and ultraviolet cameras take chemical fingerprints of the planet's gases.

Juno's magnetometers study Jupiter's deep structure by measuring its gravity and magnetic field.

LIKE THE AURORA BOREALIS ON EARTH, BEAUTIFUL LIGHT SHOWS CAN BE SEEN IN THE SKIES ABOVE JUPITER, BUT *JUNO* HAS SHOWN THEY ARE VERY DIFFERENT.

THE GREAT RED SPOT IS A STORM THAT HAS LASTED FOR AT LEAST 150 YEARS.

EXPLORING JUPITER:
GALILEO

Galileo was a mission of firsts. It was the first spacecraft to visit an asteroid, the first to observe a comet colliding with a planet, the first to orbit Jupiter and its moons, and the first to plunge into the planet. *Galileo* crashed into the gas giant to avoid a collision with its moon, Europa.

GALILEO SPECIFICATIONS

HEIGHT:
5.3m (17ft)

WEIGHT:
2,233kg (4,922lb)

POWER SOURCE:
TWO 7.8kg (17lb) BLOCKS OF PLUTONIUM

LAUNCH DATE:
18 OCTOBER 1989, FROM THE SPACE SHUTTLE *ATLANTIS*

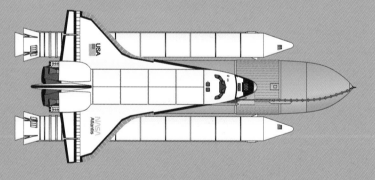

MISSION SPECIFICATIONS

DISTANCE TRAVELLED:
4.6 BILLION KM (2.8 BILLION MILES)

NUMBER OF JUPITER ORBITS: **34**

PEOPLE WHO WORKED ON THE MISSION: **800+**

MISSION DURATION: **14 YEARS**

TERMINATION: **21 SEPTEMBER 2003**

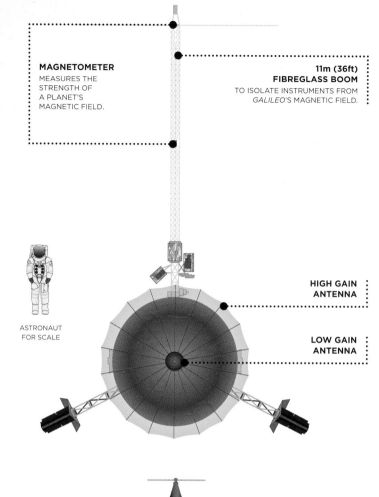

MAGNETOMETER
MEASURES THE STRENGTH OF A PLANET'S MAGNETIC FIELD.

11m (36ft) FIBREGLASS BOOM
TO ISOLATE INSTRUMENTS FROM *GALILEO*'S MAGNETIC FIELD.

ASTRONAUT FOR SCALE

HIGH GAIN ANTENNA

LOW GAIN ANTENNA

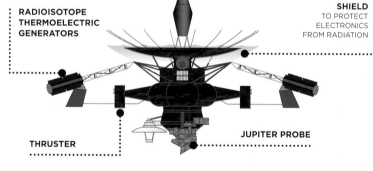

RADIOISOTOPE THERMOELECTRIC GENERATORS

SHIELD
TO PROTECT ELECTRONICS FROM RADIATION

THRUSTER

JUPITER PROBE

ENTRY PROBE

Galileo's entry probe was launched towards Jupiter's cloud tops in July 1995. The probe took five months to reach Jupiter's atmosphere and then less than an hour later it was destroyed. A heat shield protected the probe for the first few minutes before it fell away and the parachute was deployed. The probe sent a radio signal for 58 minutes before giving way to Jupiter's tremendous pressure and heat of around 13,700°C (24,700°F).

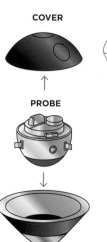

COVER

PROBE

HEAT SHIELD

PROBE DURING DESCENT

COMET DEATH

In 1994, *Galileo* was only 238 million km (147 million miles) from Jupiter when a comet called Shoemaker-Levy 9 collided with the planet. Ripped apart by the planet's tidal forces, the 2km-wide (1.2 mile) comet broke into 23 fragments. From 16 to 22 July, these fragments plummeted towards the surface at around 60km/sec (37 miles/sec) and struck with an estimated force equivalent to 300 million atomic bombs. One piece, named 'fragment G', left a scar on the surface stretching 12,000km (7456 miles).

THE AFTERMATH OF A COMET PIECE STRIKE ON JUPITER CAN BE SEEN HERE.

LONG ROUTE

In order to get up enough speed to reach Jupiter, *Galileo* had to borrow energy from other planets by carrying out gravity assists, or slingshots. *Galileo* therefore carried out a flyby of Venus and two flybys of Earth to slingshot itself to Jupiter.

GASPRA

IDA

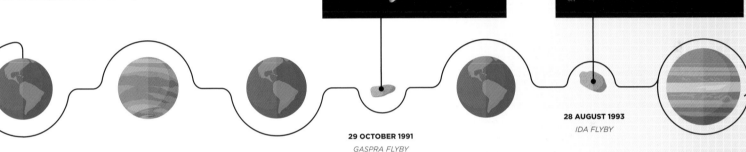

28 AUGUST 1993
IDA FLYBY

29 OCTOBER 1991
GASPRA FLYBY

18 OCTOBER 1989
LAUNCH

10 FEBRUARY 1990
VENUS FLYBY

8 DECEMBER 1990
EARTH FLYBY

8 DECEMBER 1992
EARTH FLYBY

8 DECEMBER 1995
JUPITER ORBIT

JUPITER'S MOONS

Galileo made some startling discoveries during its passes of Jupiter's four largest moons: Ganymede, Callisto, Io and Europa. It found that the icy moon Europa has a subsurface ocean that has more water than Earth and that Ganymede has its own magnetic field. Callisto also has water and an exosphere with oxygen. Most extraordinary of all was the moon Io, which contains over 400 active volcanoes that constantly blow material hundreds of kilometres into space.

THIS VOLCANIC PLUME ON IO WAS 140km (86 miles) HIGH.

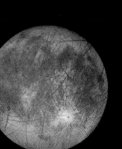

GANYMEDE

IO

EUROPA

CALLISTO

THE TRAVELLER'S GUIDE TO JUPITER

Jupiter is a gas giant. A spacecraft would be crushed and vaporised by the planet's extreme pressure and temperatures within an hour of entering the atmosphere. You should come for a flyby to see Jupiter's sights, but stay on a nearby moon.

LANDING ← - - - - - - - - - - - - →

Europa is Jupiter's nearest moon and all the rage among astronomers and scientists. This is because the *Galileo* spacecraft found evidence of a giant ocean there. Some think that there is a good chance this water may contain a simple form of alien life. However, the water is also hidden under a 15–25km (9.2–15.5 mile) thick shell of ice that covers the moon. This is both good and bad news. On the one hand, the ice is too thick to crack under the weight of a heavy lander. On the other, it will be hard to drill through to explore the ocean.

KIT BOX

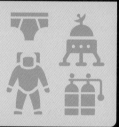

- ✓ **A LUNAR LANDER**
- ✓ **OXYGEN, FOOD AND WATER**
- ✓ **WARM SPACESUIT WITH EXTRA PROTECTION AND THERMAL UNDERWEAR**

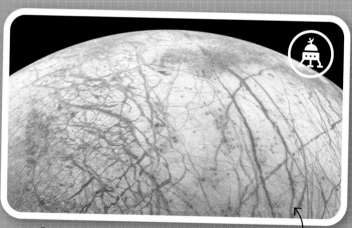

Try landing on Europa, the closest moon to Jupiter.

SURFACE ← - - - - - - - - - - - - →

Europa's icy, white surface is criss-crossed with fractures and splotchy patches of brown. The fractures can be thousands of kilometres long and 1–2km (0.6–1.25 miles) wide, so you'll need to watch your footing. There are odd, geyser-like plumes of water, which spurt many kilometres into space. Although it is not known if the water is warm, it is salty, so it will affect your spacesuit instruments if you get caught under one. Best to take your photos from a safe distance. There is some oxygen in Europa's very thin atmosphere, but not enough to breathe, so stay suited-up at all times.

EXPLORING ← - - - - - - - - - - - - →

You will need a well-insulated spacesuit with a heating system to withstand the temperatures on Europa, which range between -160°C (-320°F) and -220°C (-428°F). Your suit must also have extra protection against radioactive particles. Earthquakes and meteorites are other hazards to look out for. A must-see Europa landmark is its chaos terrain, which you'll walk to easily with only around 13% of the gravity felt on Earth. Here, the ice has been split into large, jumbled blocks, some up to 1km (0.6 miles) in height.

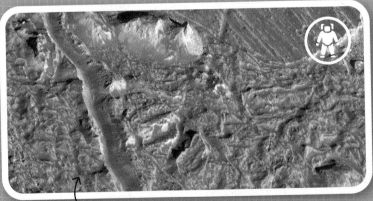

Closer view of Europa's surface.

➤ JUPITER DATA FILE

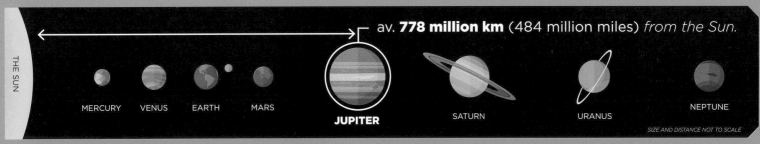

av. **778 million km** (484 million miles) *from the Sun.*

THE SUN

MERCURY VENUS EARTH MARS **JUPITER** SATURN URANUS NEPTUNE

SIZE AND DISTANCE NOT TO SCALE

➤ TEMPERATURE

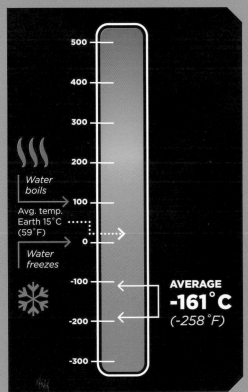

500
400
300
200
100

Water boils

Avg. temp. Earth 15°C (59°F)

0

Water freezes

-100
-200
-300

AVERAGE -161°C *(-258°F)*

➤ SIZE

EARTH

JUPITER

AVERAGE DIAMETER

142,984km
(88,846 miles)

MOONS:
79

EUROPA GANYMEDE IO CALLISTO

➤ AVERAGE SPEED

13km/sec
(8 miles/sec)

Although Jupiter is slower than Earth, it travels over 47,000km (29,000 miles) every hour.

EARTH: 30km/sec (18.5 miles/sec)

➤ CALENDAR

Length of a day
9 hours, 55 minutes

Length of a year
12 Earth years

➤ SURFACE CHARACTER

ATMOSPHERE:

There are three layers of cloud surrounding Jupiter. We can't be sure of their exact make-up yet, but it looks like the cloud closest to the planet is made of water and ice, surrounded by a layer of ammonium hydrosulfide, and then a final layer of ammonia ice crystals.

GRAVITY:

x 2.53
of EARTH

If you weigh 70kg (11st) on Earth, you will weigh 177kg (28st) on Jupiter.

H₂ HYDROGEN
90%

He HELIUM
>10%

OTHER GASES
<1%

➤ SPOTLIGHT

STORM OF THE CENTURY

Jupiter's most recognisable feature is its red spot, which is, in fact, a gigantic storm twice the size of Earth. The storm has been raging for hundreds of years and contains winds of up to 680km/h (420mph).

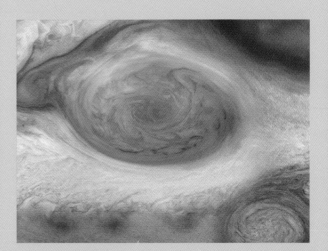

SATURN

A gas giant surrounded by sparkling ice rings, Saturn is the jewel of the Solar System. It is a wild world whipped by ferocious winds and a crushing atmosphere that can turn soot into diamonds. Saturn is hostile to humans, but over 62 moons orbit the planet, some of which may have the ingredients for life.

THE RINGS WERE DISCOVERED BY **GALILEO GALILEI** IN 1610, WHO OBSERVED THEM WITH A **TELESCOPE**.

PIONEER

When Galileo first pointed his telescope at Saturn in 1610, he reported that the planet appeared to have 'ears'. Later astronomers imagined these ears to be solid rings, or unbroken discs. It wasn't until 1979 that the spacecraft *Pioneer 11* sent back the first close-up photos of Saturn. It revealed that there were several rings, some of which contained moons. The planet itself was reported to be a bitterly cold world with an average temperature of -180°C (-356°F) and mainly composed of hydrogen.

GLOBAL COLOUR IMAGE CAPTURED BY *CASSINI* ON 23 JULY 2008.

SATURN AND TITAN (BELOW AND TO THE RIGHT) AS SEEN FROM *PIONEER 11*.

SATURN IS COVERED IN YELLOW, BROWN AND GREY CLOUDS THAT APPEAR AS **STRIPES, STREAMS** AND **WHIRLING STORMS**.

VOYAGER 1

In 1980, *Voyager 1* made some startling discoveries. It found three new moons within Saturn's rings, two of which were acting as shepherd moons. This meant their gravitational pull was keeping some of the rings perfectly in place. The rings themselves were later revealed to be made from chunks of ice – some as small as snowflakes and others as large as houses. Many of Saturn's 62 moons are also made of ice, but *Voyager 1* noticed one exception, the rocky planet-sized moon called Titan.

SATURN'S NORTHERN STORM, THE LARGEST OBSERVED BY EITHER *VOYAGER* OR *CASSINI*.

VOYAGER 2 AND BEYOND

In 1981, *Voyager 2* found a vast storm four times the size of Earth raging across Saturn's north pole. In 2017, the Lawrence Livermore National Laboratory discovered that helium droplets fall through Saturn's hydrogen-rich core. As they slow, their kinetic energy is converted to heat. This is the source of Saturn's energy, which causes its violent storms.

SATURN IS MADE LARGELY OF **GAS** AND HAS THE LOWEST DENSITY OF ANY KNOWN OBJECT IN THE SOLAR SYSTEM. IT WOULD **FLOAT IN A BATH FULL OF WATER**, IF ONE WERE FOUND TO FIT IT.

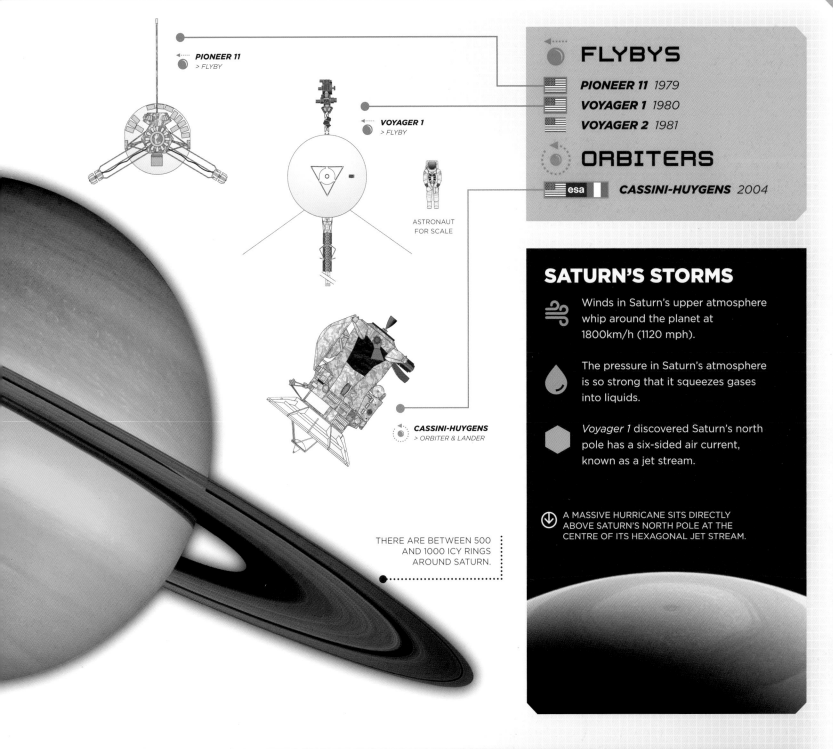

> FLYBY

PIONEER 11
> FLYBY

VOYAGER 1
> FLYBY

ASTRONAUT
FOR SCALE

FLYBYS

	PIONEER 11	1979
	VOYAGER 1	1980
	VOYAGER 2	1981

ORBITERS

esa **CASSINI-HUYGENS** 2004

CASSINI-HUYGENS
> ORBITER & LANDER

THERE ARE BETWEEN 500
AND 1000 ICY RINGS
AROUND SATURN.

SATURN'S STORMS

Winds in Saturn's upper atmosphere whip around the planet at 1800km/h (1120 mph).

The pressure in Saturn's atmosphere is so strong that it squeezes gases into liquids.

Voyager 1 discovered Saturn's north pole has a six-sided air current, known as a jet stream.

A MASSIVE HURRICANE SITS DIRECTLY ABOVE SATURN'S NORTH POLE AT THE CENTRE OF ITS HEXAGONAL JET STREAM.

SATURN'S RINGS

Saturn has seven main rings with spaces between them. They are named alphabetically after the order in which they were discovered. From the closest to the planet going out, they are called D, C, B, A, F, G and E. 'Shepherd' moons keep the dust and ice particles of the F ring in place.

EXPLORING SATURN:
CASSINI-HUYGENS

Cassini-Huygens was an extremely ambitious and complicated mission. Launched in 1997, the largest unmanned spacecraft yet constructed spent 13 years investigating Saturn and landed the *Huygens* probe onto the surface of its largest moon, Titan. This moon showed great promise: it has an atmosphere, evidence of liquid and, perhaps, the building blocks for life.

THE DESCENT

Launched from the *Cassini* spacecraft after a 6.7-year intergalactic sleep, the *Huygens* probe travelled for 4 million km (2.49 million miles) to Titan over three weeks, before landing. This is how it touched down.

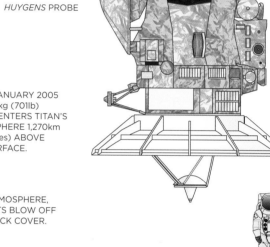

CASSINI SPACECRAFT

HUYGENS PROBE

ASTRONAUT FOR SCALE

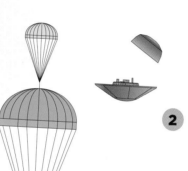

1 ON 14 JANUARY 2005 THE 318kg (701lb) PROBE ENTERS TITAN'S ATMOSPHERE 1,270km (789 miles) ABOVE THE SURFACE.

2 ONCE IN THE ATMOSPHERE, EXPLOSIVE BOLTS BLOW OFF THE PROBE'S BACK COVER.

3 A PILOT PARACHUTE IS DEPLOYED, WHICH PULLS OUT THE MAIN PARACHUTE.

4 THE FRONT SHIELD SEPARATES FROM THE PROBE.

5 THE MAIN PARACHUTE IS JETTISONED AND THE STABILISER PARACHUTE IS DEPLOYED.

6 *HUYGENS* LANDS AND THE PARACHUTE DEFLATES AND FALLS TO ONE SIDE.

⬆ AN IMAGE OF TITAN'S SURFACE TAKEN BY THE *HUYGENS* PROBE ON 14 JANUARY 2005 AS IT DESCENDED.

HUYGENS DOWN

As *Huygens* parachuted down to Titan, it beamed back photos of its surface. As first spotted by the *Cassini* flyby, they showed a world shaped by liquid, including floodplains and riverbeds. *Huygens* then photographed large boulders of ice. Titan was bitterly cold: *Huygens*' instruments showed it to be -180°C (-356°F) on its surface. This would certainly be enough to freeze water. The liquid present on Titan was later worked out to be ethane and methane. After 70 minutes, the probe's batteries ran out.

↑ ONE OF THE MANY LAKES OF LIQUID METHANE AND ETHANE FOUND ON TITAN.

⊙ CAPTURED BY *CASSINI* ON 21 MARCH 2017.

TITAN

ENCELADUS

⊙ CAPTURED BY *CASSINI* ON 10 MARCH 2012.

MOON LIFE

Although *Huygens* died, *Cassini* kept recording information about Titan as it continued to orbit. It showed that vast lakes of liquid methane and ethane were surrounded by mountains made of solid water ice. Molecules that could form complex compounds called amino acids, which give birth to life, were also detected. In around 3.5 billion years, the Sun will expand and get warmer. This will extinguish life on Earth, but warm faraway places like Titan. Who knows what could then grow there?

↑ A VIEW ACROSS ENCELADUS' SOUTH POLE TAKEN BY *CASSINI*.

SECRET ENCELADUS

Cassini had more discoveries to make from Saturn's moons. Situated on the outer edges of Saturn's rings, Enceladus is an icy moon 25 times smaller than Earth. Its many crevasses make it the most reflective object in the Solar System, but below its icy surface, the moon harboured a secret. Here, lay a liquid ocean with hot hydrothermal vents shooting plumes of water over 20km (12 miles) into space. Hydrothermal vents may have been where life first started on Earth almost 4 billion years ago, so it is possible a simple form of microbe life already exists on Enceladus.

EXPLODED PLANET

Cassini's observations of Enceladus raised an obvious question. What was heating the moon's core? Scientists think it could be the result of the gravitational pull between another larger moon, called Dione, and Saturn itself. Saturn's gravitational force is so strong that long ago it may have ripped apart an icy moon that strayed too close to the planet with the icy chunks going on to form the rings of Saturn that we see today.

→ AN ARTIST'S IMPRESSION OF THE VIEW FROM WITHIN ONE OF SATURN'S RINGS.

Saturn is mostly made up of thick, swirling gases and hot liquid with a hot solid core. What's that? You'd like to fly through Saturn like it's a cloud? The extreme temperatures and pressures will probably crush, melt and then vaporise your spacecraft. Good luck trying!

PASSING THE RING ← - - - - - - - →

The first thing you'll notice as you fly towards Saturn are its rings. They are enormous, but extremely thin. The major rings stretch outwards for 270,000km (167,000 miles) but are only 100m (328ft) thick. You'll have to be careful to navigate your spaceship through the pieces of ice that make up these rings – some are as big as a tennis ball, others the size of a barn. The widest gap between the rings is called the Cassini Division and is around 4800km (2982 miles) wide, so aim for that one!

KIT BOX

✓ **A PRESSURE-PROOF SPACECRAFT THAT CAN WITHSTAND HIGH HEAT**

✓ **A CAMERA TO SNAP SATURN'S NEVER-BEFORE-SEEN SIGHTS**

✓ **A SICK BAG FOR TURBULENT MOMENTS**

An artist's impression of a gap between Saturn's rings.

REACHING THE ATMOSPHERE

Once you've passed through Saturn's rings, expect things to get bumpy – in the upper atmosphere extreme turbulence will begin. Only a heat shield will stop you bursting into flames. If you're still alive, things outside your craft will cool as you hit Saturn's clouds. Here, temperatures drop to -170°C (-338°F), and lightning 10,000 times more powerful than on Earth will light up the ammonia clouds.

HEADING FOR THE CORE ← - - - →

As temperatures reach 30,000°C (54,000°F), lightning turns the atmosphere's methane gas into clouds of carbon soot. At around 1500km (932 miles) down, the pressure will turn the carbon soot into graphite. At 6000km (3728 miles), the pressure will turn the soot into diamonds, which pour down to a depth of 30,000km (18,600 miles) and become liquid, diamond raindrops. Things look even tougher at 40,000km (24,800 miles) into Saturn's interior. Here the pressure is so intense, that Saturn's liquid hydrogen is compressed into a hot liquid saturated with helium.

Ammonia clouds swirl above the planet.

SATURN DATA FILE

average **1.4 billion km** (886 million miles) *from the Sun.*

THE SUN

MERCURY VENUS EARTH MARS JUPITER **SATURN** URANUS NEPTUNE

SIZE AND DISTANCE NOT TO SCALE

TEMPERATURE

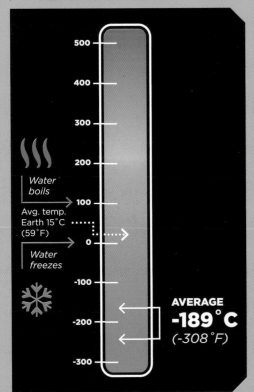

500
400
300
200
100
0
-100
-200
-300

Water boils

Avg. temp.
Earth 15°C
(59°F)

Water freezes

**AVERAGE
-189°C**
(-308°F)

SIZE

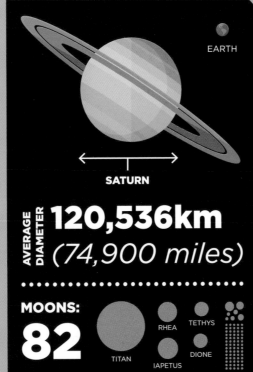

EARTH

SATURN

AVERAGE DIAMETER

120,536km
(74,900 miles)

MOONS:

82

RHEA TETHYS
TITAN DIONE
IAPETUS

AVERAGE SPEED

10km/sec
(6 miles/sec)

The third-slowest planet, Saturn's speed
is almost a third of Earth's, but it has
a lot further to travel around the Sun.

EARTH: 30km/sec (18.5 miles/sec)

CALENDAR

Length of a day
10 hours, 34 minutes

Length of a year
29 Earth years

SURFACE CHARACTER

ATMOSPHERE:

Saturn has a thick atmosphere of hydrogen,
helium, methane and ammonia. The gases
whip around at hurricane-force speeds of
500m/sec (1600ft/sec) – that's around
four-and-a-half times as fast as
the strongest winds on Earth.

GRAVITY:

x 1.07
of EARTH

If you weigh 70kg (11st)
on Earth, you will weigh
75kg (12st) on Saturn.

H₂
HYDROGEN
96%

He
HELIUM
3%

**OTHER
GASES**
1%

SPOTLIGHT

MANY MOONS

Saturn has 82 known moons and countless smaller ones.
They range in size from irregular lumps of rock, such as
Aegaeon, to planet-sized moons, such as Titan. Mimas
(below) gets a lot of attention from science-fiction fans
because of its similarity to the Death Star from *Star Wars*.

URANUS AND NEPTUNE

Far in the distant, frozen reaches of the Solar System, Uranus and Neptune hang like giant blue marbles. It is hard to imagine how far away they are. They are not just millions of kilometres away but billions. Only one Earth spacecraft has ever visited them: *Voyager 2*.

DISCOVERING THE GIANTS

The first planet to be discovered since ancient times, Uranus was identified by astronomer William Herschel in 1781. It appeared as a disc of light that Herschel thought may have been a comet. After its orbit was calculated, it was realised Herschel had found a new planet. Uranus was considered to be the most distant planet in the Solar System until 1846 when astronomers Urbain Le Verrier and Johann Galle found a similar-sized planet to Uranus over 1 million km (0.6 million miles) further out. This was Neptune.

URANUS

CAPTURED BY *VOYAGER 2* ON 14 JANUARY 1986.

VOYAGER 2

It takes a journey across at least 2.6 billion km (1.61 billion miles) of space for anything from Earth to reach Uranus. In 1986, the deep-space probe *Voyager 2* finally got close. But travelling at 17km/sec (10.5 miles/sec), it only had time to observe Uranus for six hours as it rocketed past. *Voyager*'s data was slightly underwhelming: Uranus was a blue, featureless world with an average temperature of -231°C (-448°F).

VOYAGER 2 LAUNCHED ON 20 AUGUST 1977 BEFORE *VOYAGER 1* ON 5 SEPTEMBER. THEY WERE NAMED FOR THE ORDER IN WHICH THEY WOULD REACH THEIR TARGET PLANETS.

NEPTUNE

It took *Voyager 2* nearly four more years to reach Neptune. The probe revealed another blue world, with dark spots and white methane clouds in its atmosphere. Neptune's clouds were being whipped around the planet at speeds of over 2000km/h (1200mph) – the fastest wind speeds recorded in the Solar System. The dark spots, too, represented vast, hurricane-like storms raging across the surface.

UNLIKE THE OTHER PLANETS IN THE SOLAR SYSTEM, URANUS SPINS **ON ITS SIDE**. THIS MAY HAVE HAPPENED AFTER AN OBJECT **THE SIZE OF EARTH** COLLIDED WITH IT.

ALL BAR ONE OF URANUS' MOONS ARE NAMED AFTER **CHARACTERS FROM SHAKESPEARE**. THE ONE EXCEPTION IS **UMBRIEL**, WHICH COMES FROM A POEM BY ALEXANDER POPE.

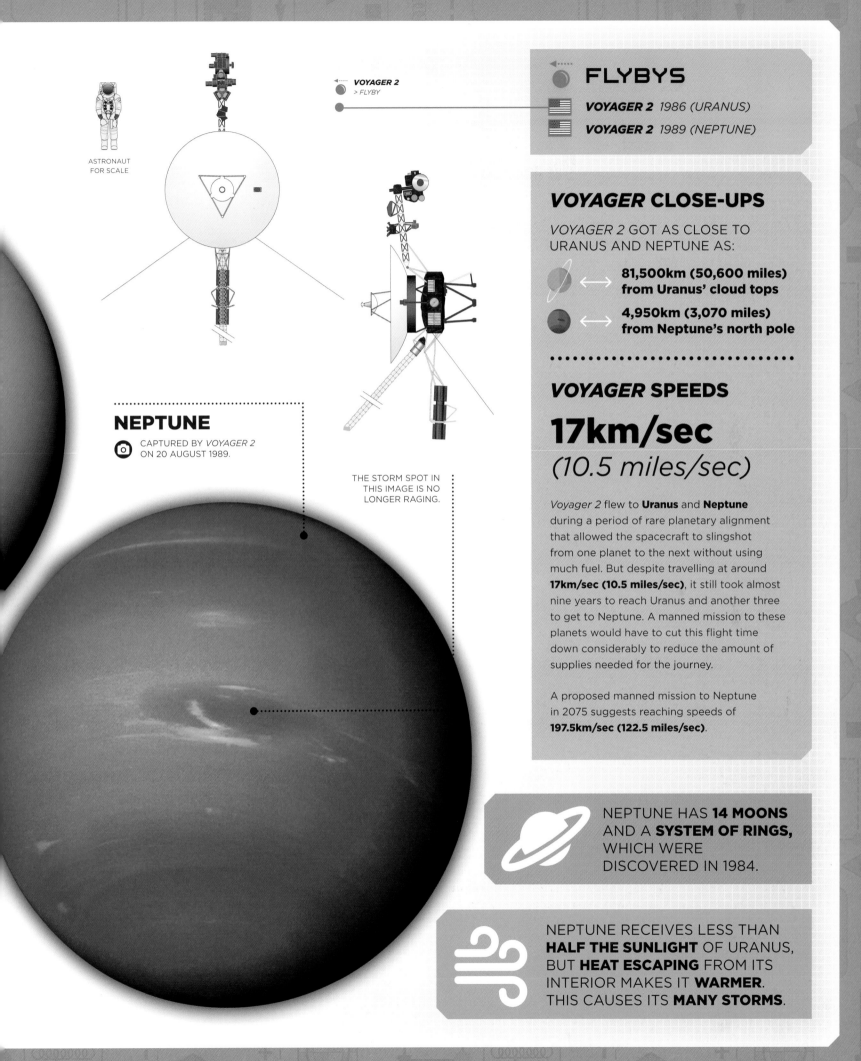

ASTRONAUT
FOR SCALE

VOYAGER 2
> FLYBY

FLYBYS

🇺🇸 **VOYAGER 2** *1986 (URANUS)*

🇺🇸 **VOYAGER 2** *1989 (NEPTUNE)*

VOYAGER CLOSE-UPS

VOYAGER 2 GOT AS CLOSE TO URANUS AND NEPTUNE AS:

**81,500km (50,600 miles)
from Uranus' cloud tops**

**4,950km (3,070 miles)
from Neptune's north pole**

VOYAGER SPEEDS

17km/sec
(10.5 miles/sec)

Voyager 2 flew to **Uranus** and **Neptune** during a period of rare planetary alignment that allowed the spacecraft to slingshot from one planet to the next without using much fuel. But despite travelling at around **17km/sec (10.5 miles/sec)**, it still took almost nine years to reach Uranus and another three to get to Neptune. A manned mission to these planets would have to cut this flight time down considerably to reduce the amount of supplies needed for the journey.

A proposed manned mission to Neptune in 2075 suggests reaching speeds of **197.5km/sec (122.5 miles/sec)**.

NEPTUNE

📷 CAPTURED BY *VOYAGER 2* ON 20 AUGUST 1989.

THE STORM SPOT IN THIS IMAGE IS NO LONGER RAGING.

NEPTUNE HAS **14 MOONS** AND A **SYSTEM OF RINGS,** WHICH WERE DISCOVERED IN 1984.

NEPTUNE RECEIVES LESS THAN **HALF THE SUNLIGHT** OF URANUS, BUT **HEAT ESCAPING** FROM ITS INTERIOR MAKES IT **WARMER.** THIS CAUSES ITS **MANY STORMS.**

THE TRAVELLER'S GUIDE TO URANUS AND NEPTUNE

Travellers wishing to visit Uranus and Neptune take note: they are a long, long way away. Voyager 2 took 12 years to visit both planets. You'll need vast amounts of food, oxygen and fuel to get there and back, plus a massive spacecraft to carry it all.

URANUS

Travellers to the gas giants Jupiter and Saturn will be familiar with conditions on Uranus. Its atmosphere is made up mainly of hydrogen and helium, with the methane that provides its blue colour. You'll probably want to find a surface to land on, but because Uranus is a gas planet, there won't be one. You'll also get tossed around in the 900km/h (560mph) winds as you descend. The temperature drops to around -221°C (-430°F) here, making it the coldest of all the planets, but the main problem is the crushing pressure which will literally squash you flat. Still, it will be an action-packed adventure until then!

KIT BOX

- ✓ OXYGEN, FOOD, WATER AND ROCKET FUEL FOR A 12-YEAR JOURNEY, AND BACK AGAIN
- ✓ PRESSURE-RESISTANT CRAFT FOR FLYING IN STRONG WINDS
- ✓ SPACESUIT WITH AN EXTRA HEATING SYSTEM FOR TRITON

Artwork of the particles in one of the rings of Uranus.

NEPTUNE

Travellers to Neptune will find it to be dark with winds that make those on Uranus seem like a gentle breeze. The atmosphere is a thick soup of hydrogen and helium with traces of other gases, covering an Earth-sized, solid core that is surrounded by a very deep hot water-ammonia ocean. The raging winds race across the planet at speeds of over 2000km/h (1200mph). These will pick you up, slam you down, and toss you around like candyfloss. So strap in tight and try to enjoy it.

TRITON

An alternative to the destructive winds of Neptune is the calmer landscape of its biggest moon, Triton. Although you'll have a solid surface to stand on, you'll have to deal with some of the coldest temperatures in the Solar System, which descend to -240°C (-460°F). Dressing warmly will seem less of a chore when you notice Triton's must-see attraction: frosty plumes of liquid nitrogen, methane and dust being blasted into the air from ice volcanoes. The plumes reach around 8km (5 miles) into the sky and then drift around 220km (140 miles) downwind – try to stay upwind.

An illustration of an ice volcano on Triton.

URANUS DATA FILE

average **2.9 billion km** (1.8 billion miles) *from the Sun.*

THE SUN

MERCURY VENUS EARTH MARS JUPITER SATURN **URANUS** NEPTUNE

SIZE AND DISTANCE NOT TO SCALE

SIZE

URANUS EARTH

AVERAGE **DIAMETER**
51,118km
(31,763 miles)

MOONS: 27

TEMPERATURE

 AVERAGE
-220°C
(-364°F)

GRAVITY

x 0.91
of EARTH

SPEED

7km/sec
(4 miles/sec)

CALENDAR

Length of a day
17 hours, 14 minutes
....
Length of a year
84 Earth years

NEPTUNE DATA FILE

average **4.5 billion km** (2.8 billion miles) *from the Sun.*

THE SUN

MERCURY VENUS EARTH MARS JUPITER SATURN URANUS **NEPTUNE**

SIZE AND DISTANCE NOT TO SCALE

SIZE

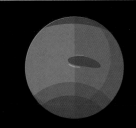

NEPTUNE EARTH

AVERAGE **DIAMETER**
49,532km
(30,779 miles)

MOONS: 14 TRITON

TEMPERATURE

 AVERAGE
-218°C
(-360°F)

GRAVITY

x 1.14
of EARTH

SPEED

5km/sec
(3 miles/sec)

CALENDAR

Length of a day
16 hours, 7 minutes
....
Length of a year
165 Earth years

PLUTO
AND THE OUTER SOLAR SYSTEM

Pluto is a frozen world that was little more than a blip in a telescope lens before *New Horizons'* flyby. *New Horizons* revealed Pluto to have mountains, gorges and glaciers with vast, icy plains patterned like alligator skin.

PLUTO CAPTURED BY *NEW HORIZONS* ON 14 JULY 2015.

SPOTTING PLUTO

In 1930, an American astronomer called Clyde Tombaugh spotted Pluto using a 33cm (13in) telescope. Initially classified as the ninth planet in the Solar System, the International Astronomical Union reclassified Pluto as a dwarf planet in 2006, in recognition that it was a smaller body and part of the Kuiper Belt, a band of ice and rock fragments left over from the formation of the Solar System.

NEW HORIZONS

Launched from Cape Canaveral, *New Horizons* began its epic voyage to Pluto in 2006. Travelling at 16km/sec (9.9 miles/sec), *New Horizons* reached Jupiter in just over a year, where it received a gravity boost from the gas giant. It then shut down all of its non-essential systems and went into hibernation for most of its eight-year voyage. Then, in 2015, the spacecraft awoke. It had reached Pluto without incident and began beaming back photos of this faraway world.

THE PROBE, WHICH COST AROUND USD$700 MILLION, IS ABOUT THE SIZE OF A GRAND PIANO.

PLUTO'S HEART

New Horizons showed Pluto to have a surface of frozen nitrogen, featuring mountains and crevasses, as well as a vast plain, also of nitrogen, 1590km (990 miles) across. Nicknamed Pluto's Heart, this plain includes a patch of smooth icy ground, called Sputnik Planitia, which has an intricate scaled pattern over the top. Scientists believe heat rising from beneath the surface created this pattern, but what is causing the heat is unknown. Some believe a liquid ocean may lie below the ice.

CLYDE TOMBAUGH, WHO **DISCOVERED** PLUTO, SAID HE'D LOVE TO VISIT THE PLANETS IN THE SOLAR SYSTEM AND AROUND OTHER STARS. *NEW HORIZONS* CARRIED OUT HIS WISH – SOME OF **HIS ASHES ARE ONBOARD**.

PLUTO FACTS

DIAMETER:
2377km (1477 miles)

MOONS:
5

AVERAGE DISTANCE FROM THE SUN:
5.9 billion km (3.66 billion miles)

LENGTH OF A DAY:
153.3 hours

LENGTH OF A YEAR:
248 years

SURFACE TEMPERATURE:
AROUND -228°C (-101°F)

PLUTO HAS AN ATMOSPHERE MADE MAINLY OF **NITROGEN**, WITH SMALL AMOUNTS OF **METHANE, CARBON MONOXIDE** AND **HYDROGEN CYANIDE**.

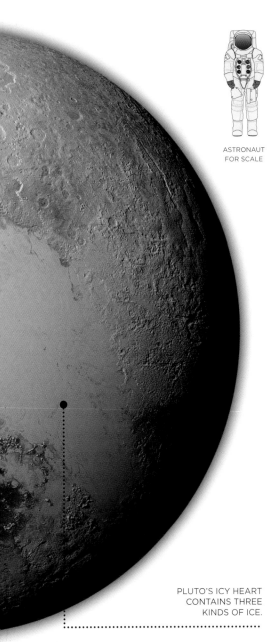

NEW HORIZONS
> FLYBY

◀····· FLYBYS

NEW HORIZONS *2015–19*

ASTRONAUT
FOR SCALE

CHARON CAPTURED BY
NEW HORIZONS IN 2015.

CHARON

As part of its flyby of Pluto, *New Horizons* sent back data about one of its moons, Charon. It revealed Charon to be covered in a belt of mountains, fractures and canyons around 1600km (994 miles) wide and stretching across the entire face of the moon. Scientists think this may have been the result of a catastrophic geological event that involved frozen ice cracking the surface open.

ULTIMA THULE

A year after its flyby of Pluto and its moons, *New Horizons* began the second part of its mission – to explore the objects of the Kuiper Belt. In January 2019, it sent back the first photos of 486958 Arrokoth, aka Ultima Thule, a strangely shaped rock and the furthest object yet visited. The red Ultima Thule's snowman shape is thought to have been formed when two smaller ball-shaped rocks merged.

PLUTO'S ICY HEART
CONTAINS THREE
KINDS OF ICE.

KUIPER BELT

Pluto is found in this doughnut-shaped ring formed of millions of icy objects. It is believed to be one of the sources of comets.

ASTEROID BELT

KUIPER BELT

INNER PLANETS

OUTER PLANETS

PLUTO

VOYAGING BEYOND THE SOLAR SYSTEM

Voyager 1 and *2* are two probes that have travelled further into space than any other human-made object. The spacecraft crossed the outer edge of our Solar System several years ago. Now, the *Voyagers* are travelling through interstellar space. It is not known when their journeys will end, or where.

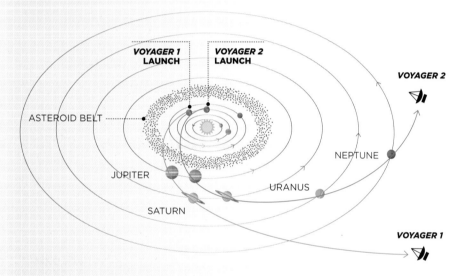

VOYAGER 1 LAUNCH
VOYAGER 2 LAUNCH
VOYAGER 2
ASTEROID BELT
NEPTUNE
JUPITER
URANUS
SATURN
VOYAGER 1

VOYAGER DISCOVERIES

DISCOVERED 22 NEW SATELLITES:
- ●●● 3 AT JUPITER
- ●●● 3 AT SATURN
- ●●●●●●●●●● 10 AT URANUS
- ●●●●●● 6 AT NEPTUNE

FOUND TRITON HAD AN ATMOSPHERE AND GEYSER-LIKE PLUMES.

OBSERVED LARGE-SCALE STORMS ON NEPTUNE.

FOUND JUPITER'S MOON IO HAS ACTIVE VOLCANOES.

SOLAR SYSTEM SLINGSHOT

Voyager 1 and *2* were launched to take advantage of a rare alignment of the planets that occurs only once every 176 years. This enabled them to harness the gravity of each planet in a slingshot manoeuvre that swung them from one planet to the next in a row. Although both spacecraft were destined for interstellar space, they followed slightly different trajectories and so reached this region at different times.

VOYAGING THROUGH TIME AND SPACE

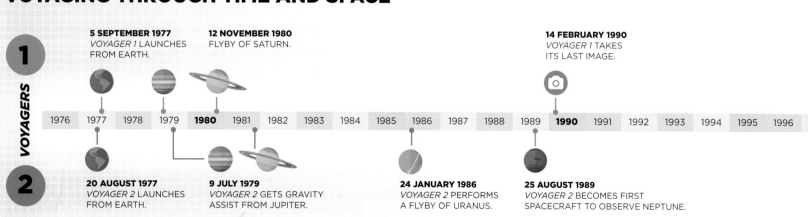

1

5 SEPTEMBER 1977
VOYAGER 1 LAUNCHES FROM EARTH.

12 NOVEMBER 1980
FLYBY OF SATURN.

14 FEBRUARY 1990
VOYAGER 1 TAKES ITS LAST IMAGE.

VOYAGERS

| 1976 | 1977 | 1978 | 1979 | **1980** | 1981 | 1982 | 1983 | 1984 | 1985 | 1986 | 1987 | 1988 | 1989 | **1990** | 1991 | 1992 | 1993 | 1994 | 1995 | 1996 |

2

20 AUGUST 1977
VOYAGER 2 LAUNCHES FROM EARTH.

9 JULY 1979
VOYAGER 2 GETS GRAVITY ASSIST FROM JUPITER.

24 JANUARY 1986
VOYAGER 2 PERFORMS A FLYBY OF URANUS.

25 AUGUST 1989
VOYAGER 2 BECOMES FIRST SPACECRAFT TO OBSERVE NEPTUNE.

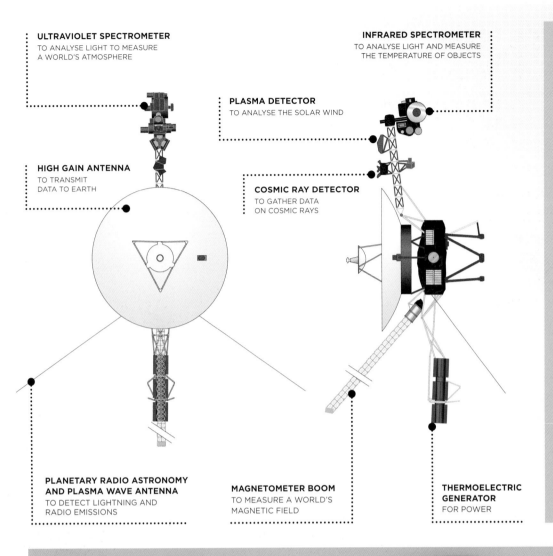

ULTRAVIOLET SPECTROMETER
TO ANALYSE LIGHT TO MEASURE
A WORLD'S ATMOSPHERE

INFRARED SPECTROMETER
TO ANALYSE LIGHT AND MEASURE
THE TEMPERATURE OF OBJECTS

PLASMA DETECTOR
TO ANALYSE THE SOLAR WIND

HIGH GAIN ANTENNA
TO TRANSMIT
DATA TO EARTH

COSMIC RAY DETECTOR
TO GATHER DATA
ON COSMIC RAYS

**PLANETARY RADIO ASTRONOMY
AND PLASMA WAVE ANTENNA**
TO DETECT LIGHTNING AND
RADIO EMISSIONS

MAGNETOMETER BOOM
TO MEASURE A WORLD'S
MAGNETIC FIELD

**THERMOELECTRIC
GENERATOR**
FOR POWER

VOYAGER 2 SPECIFICATIONS

WEIGHT: **721.9kg (1591lb)**

HEIGHT: **47cm (18.5in)**

LENGTH: **1.78m (5.8ft)**

VOYAGER 1 STATS

DISTANCE FROM EARTH:
22.2 billion km (13.8 billion miles)

MISSION LENGTH SO FAR:
42 YEARS, 5 MONTHS, 7 DAYS

SPEED:
61,197km/h (38,026mph)

VOYAGER 2 STATS

DISTANCE FROM EARTH:
18.5 billion km (11.5 billion miles)

MISSION LENGTH SO FAR:
42 YEARS, 5 MONTHS, 23 DAYS

SPEED:
55,345km/h (34,390mph)

FIGURES AS OF 13 FEBRUARY 2020.

GOLD RECORDS

Because it was not known where *Voyager 1* and *2*
might end up, a gold record was included with
each spacecraft to explain life on Earth to any
aliens that find them. They contain images and
sounds from Earth, including greetings in 55
languages and music by popular and classical
performers. Accompanying the records is a record
player and instructions on how to play them.

THE RECORD'S COVER (LEFT) FEATURES SEVERAL
DIAGRAMS, INCLUDING INSTRUCTIONS ON HOW TO
USE THE RECORD AND THE LOCATION OF OUR SUN.

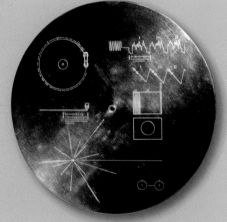

17 FEBRUARY 1998
VOYAGER 1 BECOMES MOST DISTANT
HUMAN-MADE OBJECT IN SPACE.

15 DECEMBER 2004
VOYAGER 1 CROSSES THE TERMINATION
SHOCK, THE EDGE OF THE SOLAR SYSTEM.

25 AUGUST 2012
VOYAGER 1 ENTERS
INTERSTELLAR SPACE.

1999 **2000** 2001 2002 2003 2004 2005 2006 2007 2008 2009 **2010** 2011 2012 2013 2014 2015 2016 2017 2018 2019 **2020**

5 SEPTEMBER 2007
VOYAGER 2 CROSSES
TERMINATION SHOCK.

5 NOVEMBER 2018
VOYAGER 2 REACHES
INTERSTELLAR SPACE.

THE SUN

THE SUN CAPTURED BY THE *SOLAR AND HELIOSPHERIC OBSERVATORY (SOHO)* ON 20 JUNE 2013.

A massive ball of hot burning gases, the Sun is Earth's most important celestial neighbour. It provides the energy that allows all life on our planet to exist, but is also violent and variable, expelling flares, radiation, the solar wind and coronal mass ejections. Missions investigating the effects of the Sun on the planets are of great importance.

SOHO

The ESA and NASA's *Solar and Heliospheric Observatory (SOHO)* was launched in 1995 to orbit around 1.5 million km (930,000 miles) from Earth. *SOHO* has photographed coronal mass ejections and sunspots. It has also enabled the discovery of thousands more comets seen passing close to the Sun. Roughly half of all known comets have been spotted by people searching *SOHO* images online.

A CORONAL MASS EJECTION (CME), A SOLAR PHENOMENON THAT CAN SEND BILLIONS OF TONS OF PARTICLES INTO SPACE THAT CAN REACH EARTH IN ONE TO THREE DAYS.

HINODE

In 2006, Japan's *Hinode* satellite was sent to investigate the Sun's extremely hot outer atmosphere, called the corona. Scientists hope the satellite's data will help explain why the temperature of the Sun's corona is millions of degrees centigrade, while its surface is only around 5500°C (9932°F). The mission is expected to end in 2022.

IRIS

The *Interface Region Imaging Spectrograph (IRIS)* was launched in 2013 to examine the Sun's chromosphere. This is the second of three layers in the Sun's atmosphere, which sends solar material into the corona and blasts ultraviolet radiation to Earth. In 2016, *Iris* found that solar 'bombs' were moving through the Sun's atmosphere to its corona, which might help explain why it is so hot.

IT TAKES JUST OVER **EIGHT MINUTES** FOR LIGHT TO REACH EARTH FROM THE SUN.

THE FIRST IMAGE TAKEN BY THE *PARKER SOLAR PROBE* FROM INSIDE THE SUN'S ATMOSPHERE. THE BRIGHT DOT IS MERCURY.

PARKER SOLAR PROBE

Launched in 2018, the *Parker Solar Probe* will travel as close as 6.1 million km (3.7 million miles) to the Sun's photosphere (its visible surface) in 2025. This is closer to the Sun than any spacecraft has travelled before. The probe will make periodic passes of the Sun over seven years to provide never-before-seen views of its corona and investigate the origin of its solar wind.

THE SUN IS AMOST **HALFWAY** THROUGH ITS LIFE. IT HAS BURNED OFF AROUND **HALF** OF ITS HYDROGEN STORES, BUT HAS ENOUGH LEFT FOR ANOTHER **5 BILLION YEARS**.

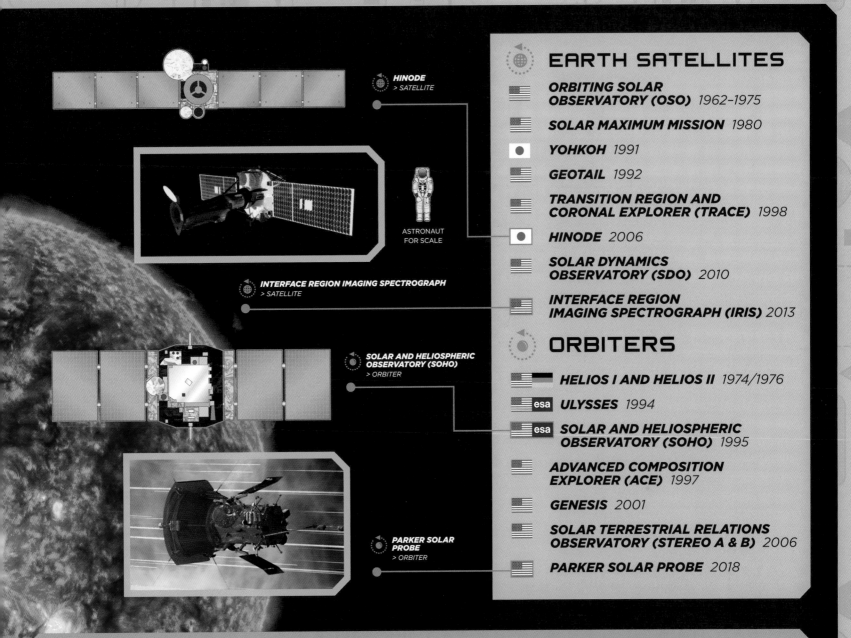

HINODE
> SATELLITE

ASTRONAUT
FOR SCALE

INTERFACE REGION IMAGING SPECTROGRAPH
> SATELLITE

SOLAR AND HELIOSPHERIC OBSERVATORY (SOHO)
> ORBITER

PARKER SOLAR PROBE
> ORBITER

EARTH SATELLITES

ORBITING SOLAR OBSERVATORY (OSO) *1962-1975*

SOLAR MAXIMUM MISSION *1980*

YOHKOH *1991*

GEOTAIL *1992*

TRANSITION REGION AND CORONAL EXPLORER (TRACE) *1998*

HINODE *2006*

SOLAR DYNAMICS OBSERVATORY (SDO) *2010*

INTERFACE REGION IMAGING SPECTROGRAPH (IRIS) *2013*

ORBITERS

HELIOS I AND HELIOS II *1974/1976*

esa **ULYSSES** *1994*

esa **SOLAR AND HELIOSPHERIC OBSERVATORY (SOHO)** *1995*

ADVANCED COMPOSITION EXPLORER (ACE) *1997*

GENESIS *2001*

SOLAR TERRESTRIAL RELATIONS OBSERVATORY (STEREO A & B) *2006*

PARKER SOLAR PROBE *2018*

THE TRAVELLER'S GUIDE TO THE SUN

The two pressing problems preventing manned missions to the Sun are fuel and heat. The Sun is around 150 million km (93 million miles) away and we haven't yet invented a spacecraft that can carry enough fuel to get you and your supplies there and back, but the main problem is temperature. The heat on the Sun's surface is around 5500°C (9900°F), which will melt you and your spaceship instantly. How about a nice jaunt to the Moon instead?

AGE: **4.5 BILLION YEARS**

STAR TYPE: **YELLOW DWARF**

COMPOSITION: **HYDROGEN AND HELIUM**

AVERAGE DIAMETER:
1,390,473km (863,999 miles)

TEMPERATURE AT SUN'S CORE:
15,000,000°C (27,000,000°F)

1.3 MILLION EARTHS COULD FIT INSIDE THE SUN

THE SUN MAKES UP 99.8 % OF THE MASS OF THE ENTIRE SOLAR SYSTEM

IT TAKES THE SUN APPROXIMATELY 230 MILLION YEARS TO COMPLETE ONE ORBIT OF THE CENTRE OF THE MILKY WAY

THE SUN

MERCURY
VENUS
EARTH
MARS
JUPITER
SATURN
URANUS
NEPTUNE
PLUTO

SMALLER BODIES:
ASTEROIDS

When the planets formed, some chunks of rock called asteroids were left over. Most are in a region called the Asteroid Belt, which lies between Mars and Jupiter, but sometimes an asteroid is knocked off course. One such asteroid caused a mass extinction on Earth, wiping out the dinosaurs around 66 million years ago.

GALILEO TO GASPRA

The *Galileo* probe provided the first close-up study of asteroids while en route to Jupiter. In 1991, *Galileo* passed asteroid 951 Gaspra at a distance of 1600km (1000 miles). Its photos revealed Gaspra to have hundreds of small craters.

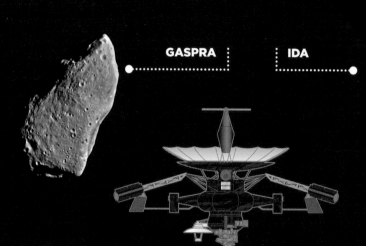

GASPRA

IDA

🇺🇸 *GALILEO* PROBE

IDA IS ONE OF MANY ASTEROIDS TO HAVE A MOON OF ITS OWN. DACTYL IS JUST 1.5km (0.9 miles) WIDE.

ASTEROID STRIKES

In September 2019, an asteroid around the size of a tall building zoomed past Earth at a speed of 23,000km/h (14,000mph). Although passing at a distance of 5.3 million km (3.3 million miles), asteroid 2000 QW7 was defined as a Near Earth Object – something that comes within 200 million km (124 million miles) of the planet. The asteroid was over 650m (2100ft) long, which is more than 30 times smaller than the asteroid that killed off the dinosaurs.

⬆ IT IS BELIEVED THAT THE DINOSAURS WERE WIPED OUT AFTER AN ASTEROID HIT THE YUCATÁN PENINSULA IN MEXICO 66 MILLION YEARS AGO.

EROS

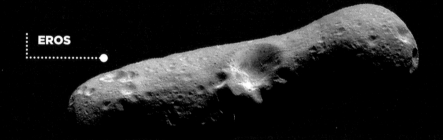

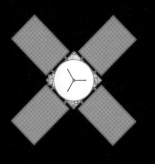

🇺🇸 *NEAR SHOEMAKER* PROBE

NEAR TO EROS

The *Near Earth Asteroid Rendezvous Shoemaker* (*NEAR*) probe was the first spacecraft designed solely to investigate an asteroid – Eros – and gather information about its physical make-up. In 2000, *NEAR Shoemaker* dropped into orbit around Eros and photographed the asteroid from a distance of around 1200km (740 miles). It discovered Eros had hundreds of craters and a density similar to Earth's..

🇺🇸 ***DAWN* PROBE**

***DAWN* TO VESTA**

Launched in 2007, *Dawn* was a probe of many firsts on its 6.9 billion km (4.9 billion mile) mission. In 2011, *Dawn* became the first spacecraft to orbit an asteroid in the Asteroid Belt. This was Vesta, the second largest object in the belt. In 2015, *Dawn* went into orbit around the dwarf planet Ceres, the largest object in the Asteroid Belt.

VESTA

CERES

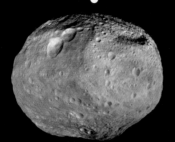

ITOKAWA

AN ARTIST'S IMPRESSION OF *HAYABUSA* TAKING A SAMPLE FROM ITOKAWA'S SURFACE BEFORE RETURNING TO EARTH.

HAYABUSA TO ITOKAWA

Launched in 2003, the Japanese *Hayabusa* probe was sent to land on the near-Earth asteroid 25143 Itokawa and collect rock samples to bring back to Earth. It did so in 2010, while also recording data on the asteroid's shape, composition and density. A new probe, *Hayabusa 2*, went one step further in 2019 by completing two successful touchdowns on asteroid 162173 Ryugu and collecting samples. This involved firing explosive bullets from *Hayabusa 2*'s sampling arm into Ryugu, which loosened enough rocky material to then scoop up.

⬤ ***HAYABUSA* PROBE**

HOW BIG?

Asteroids vary wildly in shape and size. Ceres (the biggest) is a quarter of the size of our Moon – that's roughly the same size as Texas!

VESTA

CERES

TEXAS

ITOKAWA   **RYUGU**   **EROS**   **IDA**   **GASPRA**

SMALLER BODIES:
COMETS

Comets are huge chunks of ice and rock that visit from the outer Solar System. As a comet gets closer to the Sun, some of its ice starts to turn to vapour. This creates a 'tail' of vapour, gas and dust. Some comets are regular visitors to the Earth, such as Halley's Comet, which passes by every 75 years.

⬆ HALLEY'S COMET WAS SAID TO HAVE INSPIRED WILLIAM THE CONQUEROR. THE COMET IS SHOWN ON THE BAYEUX TAPESTRY, WHICH RECORDED HIS 1066 INVASION.

GIOTTO'S POTATO

Edmond Halley (1656–1742) was an English astronomer who believed that a particular comet had passed by Earth at regular intervals for many centuries. Records revealed a bright comet being mentioned in 240BCE, 1066CE and 1301CE. Halley predicted it would return again in 1758. He was right. When the subsequently named Halley's Comet flew past in 1986, an armada of probes was launched after it. The European Space Agency's *Giotto* passed 596km (370 miles) from the comet and photographed it.

HALLEY'S COMET

PHOTOS SHOWED THE COMET TO BE DARK, POTATO-SHAPED AND AROUND 15km (9.3 miles) ACROSS.

esa *GIOTTO* PROBE

esa *ROSETTA* PROBE

ROSETTA PROBE

Rosetta was a European Space Agency probe launched in 2004 to study the comet 67P/Churyumov-Gerasimenko. There was great anticipation about the mission: comets are of interest because they are ancient bodies left over from the formation of the Solar System. It was hoped, therefore, that when *Rosetta* arrived at 67P/Churyumov-Gerasimenko in 2014 it would unlock secrets about the history of the Solar System. To explore further, *Rosetta* launched a lander called *Philae* onto the comet's surface.

67P/CHURYUMOV-GERASIMENKO

67P/CHURYUMOV-GERASIMENKO IS ROUGHLY 3km x 5km (1.9 miles x 3.1 miles).

BURJ KHALIFA, THE TALLEST BUILDING ON EARTH, FOR SCALE

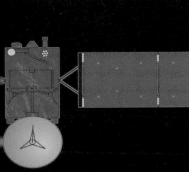

PHILAE'S LANDING

The 100kg (220lb) *Philae* was the first lander to visit a comet. But landing on 67P/Churyumov-Gerasimenko proved to be a vastly difficult task. To gain a foothold, *Philae* was designed to fire harpoons into the comet's surface; but these failed. When it tried to touch down anyway, *Philae* bounced off the comet's icy surface and landed on its side in the shadow of a cliff. This meant the lander was unable to charge its solar batteries, which drained after a few hours.

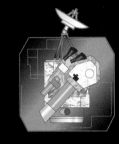

esa **PHILAE LANDER**

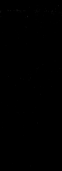

DEEP IMPACT PROBE

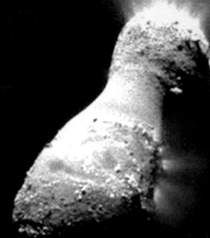

9P/TEMPEL 1

DEEP IMPACT

The *Deep Impact* mission consisted of two parts: a coffee-table-sized spacecraft and a smaller probe that was designed to crash onto comet 9P/Tempel 1. The probe crashed into the comet with an impact equivalent to 4.17 tonnes (4.1 tons) of dynamite. This left a crater around 150m (490ft) wide, which revealed the pristine untouched material inside. This showed that beneath their surface, comets have a fluffy texture with sections of empty space.

STARDUST COLLECTION

Stardust was a US probe launched to collect dust from a comet and return it to Earth. In 2002, the spacecraft flew past and studied the asteroid 5535 Annefrank before continuing to the comet 81P/Wild in 2004. To collect the dust, *Stardust* used a long, folded arm with a sponge-like material called aerogel at the end. After it landed back on Earth in 2014, the material *Stardust* had collected proved to be of great interest. The dust contained the amino acid glycine, one of the chemical compounds found in living things.

STARDUST PROBE

 CLOSE-UP OF THE TRACKS MADE BY COMET PARTICLES IN AEROGEL.

Comets and asteroids are predicted to be favourite, must-see space destinations. After all, there are lots of them and they often travel close to Earth. This means you can have a small space adventure without all those long, tedious journeys. So, get ready to jump aboard!

LANDING ← - - - - - - - - - - - - - - - →

The tricky part is catching up with comets or asteroids – they travel for millions of kilometres through space and are fast. Really fast. Often, they hit speeds of around 18km/sec (11 miles/sec) as they approach the Sun. This will require you to reach a similar speed and pull up alongside your chosen comet or asteroid. To do this, you could try a new technique called a 'gravity tractor'. This involves using the gravity caused by your spacecraft to get alongside a comet or asteroid before launching your lander to the surface.

KIT BOX

✓ **HARPOONS, ROPES AND TETHERS**

✓ **SPACESUIT WITH HEATING, COOLING AND RADIATION PROTECTION**

✓ **A BUCKET AND SPADE TO COLLECT SAMPLES**

The surface of comet 67P/Churyumov–Gerasimenko.

SURFACE ← - - - - - - - - - - - - - - - →

You'll need to shoot some sharp, tethered harpoons into the surface; otherwise your lander will probably just bounce off. Once your harpoons are in and you've winched your lander down, it's time to have a look around. For this you'll need a spacesuit with extra heating and cooling systems. When the *Giotto* probe visited Halley's Comet, the surface temperature was 77°C (170.6°F). However, when the *Philae* lander touched down on comet 67P/Churyumov-Gerasimenko, the temperature was -70°C (-158°F).

EXPLORING ← - - - - - - - - - - - - - - - →

Comets and asteroids do not have atmospheres, so there is nothing to stop radioactive particles bombarding you. Your spacesuit will need some serious radiation protection. Also prepare for a gravity surprise. Spherical objects like Earth use gravity to pull everything down to their surface. But comets and asteroids often have irregular shapes, meaning you might be pulled to the side as well. The strength of the gravity will vary according to the size of the comet or asteroid, but it will almost certainly be less than on Earth.

The comet Hale-Bopp seen in 1997

➤ ASTEROIDS AND COMETS DATA FILE

All asteroids orbit the Sun in short elliptical orbits.

Most asteroids are found in the Asteroid Belt, which is located between the orbits of Mars and Jupiter.

Comets usually have long, elongated elliptical orbits.

Comets are believed to originate in either the Kuiper Belt or the Oort Cloud, an area of icy bodies thought to exist in the far reaches of the Solar System.

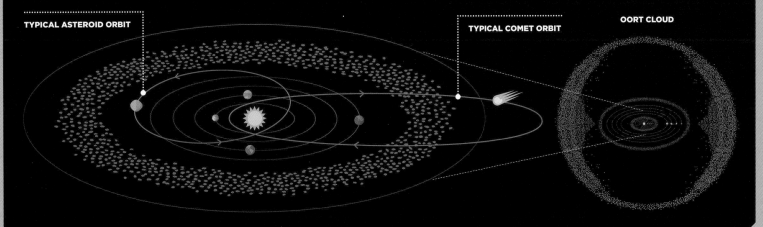

TYPICAL ASTEROID ORBIT

TYPICAL COMET ORBIT

OORT CLOUD

➤ ASTEROIDS

Mainly made of silicate-based rock, asteroids also contain metals such as iron and nickel.

Smaller rocky objects are known as meteoroids. If one reaches Earth, it will normally burn up in the atmosphere as a meteor or 'shooting star'.

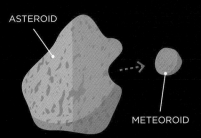

ASTEROID

METEOROID

There are 188 million known asteroids in the Solar System and more are being discovered all the time. Over 757,600 asteroids were discovered in 2018 alone.

On 30 June 1908, an asteroid estimated to have a diameter of anything between 60m and 1000m (200–3200ft) entered Earth's atmosphere over Siberia and exploded above the Tunguska River. The blast flattened trees (left) and caused an earthquake that was felt over 40km (25 miles) away.

A Tunguska-type event is rare, but an asteroid the size of a car falls into Earth's atmosphere on average once every year. A bright fireball will fly through the skies, but usually burns up before hitting the ground.

➤ COMETS

Nicknamed 'dirty snowballs' or 'cosmic snowballs', comets are composed of ice mixed with dust.

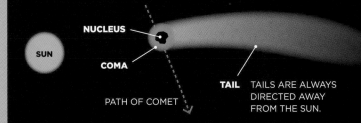

SUN

NUCLEUS

COMA

PATH OF COMET

TAIL — TAILS ARE ALWAYS DIRECTED AWAY FROM THE SUN.

A comet is made up of:

NUCLEUS A solid centre of ice, rock, gas and dust.
COMA A fuzzy mix of carbon dioxide, ammonia, dust and water vapour around the nucleus.
TAIL A long stream of ions, gas and dust.

Most comets have two tails – a dust tail and a gas tail, as in the image of Hale-Bopp on the opposite page.

Because they are bright and reflective and have long tails, comets are among the most spectacular objects in the sky.

Some comets have an orbital period of millions of years. This means there are many comets that have passed by Earth, but humans have never seen them.

There are over 3500 known comets to date, but scientists believe there are billions of bodies in the Kuiper Belt and Oort Cloud that could one day become comets.

THE UNIVERSE

It is almost impossible to imagine there are at least 4.3 billion km (2.7 billion miles) between Earth and Neptune. But this distance is nothing compared to the vastness of space. Its size is unimaginable. Earth is just a speck in the open blackness of the Universe dotted with stars, galaxies and dust. Breaking the Universe down to its parts is the best way to think about it.

HOW BIG?

EARTH

Our home is a ball of rock averaging 12,756km (7,926 miles) across. It has air to breathe and is the only planet we know of that can support life.

THE SOLAR SYSTEM

Earth is one of eight planets orbiting the Sun in our Solar System. The furthest planet, Neptune, is 4.5 billion km (2.8 billion miles) from the Sun.

THE MILKY WAY

Our Sun is only one of over 100 billion stars grouped together into a galaxy we call the Milky Way. It would take a beam of light travelling at 300,000km/sec (186,000 miles/sec) 100,000 years to travel from one side of the Milky Way to the other.

GALAXY SHAPES

The Milky Way is a spiral-shaped galaxy, but other galaxies have different shapes. There are four main types of galaxy shape: elliptical, spiral, lenticular and irregular. There are probably others we don't yet know about.

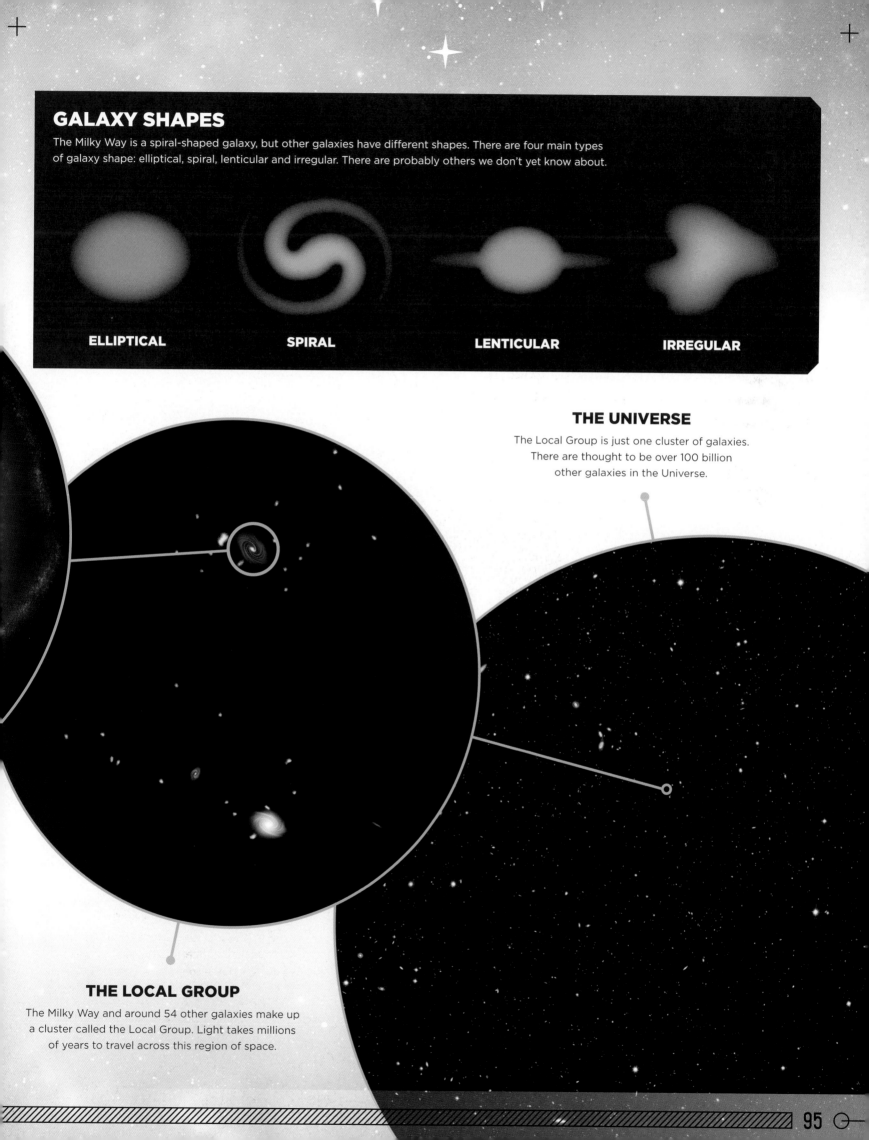

ELLIPTICAL

SPIRAL

LENTICULAR

IRREGULAR

THE UNIVERSE

The Local Group is just one cluster of galaxies. There are thought to be over 100 billion other galaxies in the Universe.

THE LOCAL GROUP

The Milky Way and around 54 other galaxies make up a cluster called the Local Group. Light takes millions of years to travel across this region of space.

SPACE TELESCOPES

Traditional telescopes were placed in high locations on Earth to be away from light pollution. But with the arrival of space exploration, telescopes could be launched into space. Here, above the atmosphere, they have a clear, unobstructed view of the Universe.

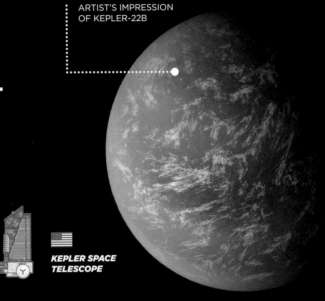

ARTIST'S IMPRESSION OF KEPLER-22B

KEPLER SPACE TELESCOPE

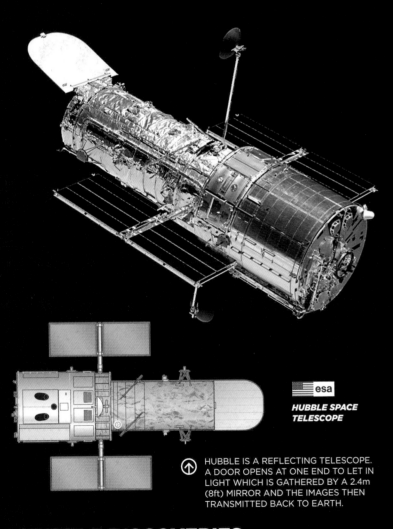

esa

HUBBLE SPACE TELESCOPE

HUBBLE IS A REFLECTING TELESCOPE. A DOOR OPENS AT ONE END TO LET IN LIGHT WHICH IS GATHERED BY A 2.4m (8ft) MIRROR AND THE IMAGES THEN TRANSMITTED BACK TO EARTH.

KEPLER'S NEW WORLDS

Launched into the Sun's orbit in 2009, the Kepler space telescope was designed to locate exoplanets – planets in solar systems other than our own. To do this, Kepler watched for the telltale dimming that occurs when planets pass in front of their suns. The thousands of exoplanets discovered by the telescope include gas giants, ice giants and super-hot rock planets. One planet called Kepler-22b, which is about twice the diameter of Earth, was the first to be located in the habitable 'goldilocks' zone – so called because it's the region where liquid water can exist (not too hot, not too cold).

HUBBLE DISCOVERIES

In 1990 Space Shuttle *Discovery* delivered the Hubble Space Telescope (HST) into orbit around 600km (372 miles) above Earth. Hubble's discoveries have revolutionised the way we see the cosmos. Its photos have included new stars, dying stars and even exploding stars (supernovas). One image revealed 1500 new galaxies in a never-before-seen corner of the Universe. Hubble's observations have helped scientists understand the Universe in exciting new ways.

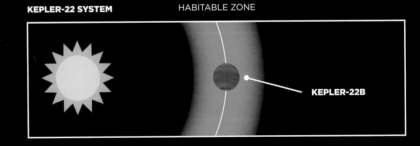

KEPLER-22 SYSTEM   HABITABLE ZONE

KEPLER-22B

SOLAR SYSTEM   HABITABLE ZONE

EARTH

THE NEW JAMES WEBB

Due to launch in the 2020s as the successor to the Hubble Space Telescope, the James Webb Space Telescope (JWST) is designed to study the Universe's first galaxies. It will also detect infrared light given out by collapsing clouds of gas and dust that will become stars. Devised to orbit around the Sun, the JWST will employ a mirror 6.5m (21ft) in diameter, which is seven times the size of Hubble's.

⊘ THE JWST IS TOO LARGE TO FIT INSIDE ANY CURRENT SPACECRAFT, SO HAS BEEN BUILT WITH A HINGED MIRROR AND SUN SHIELD THAT WILL UNFOLD ONCE IT HAS BEEN DELIVERED INTO SPACE.

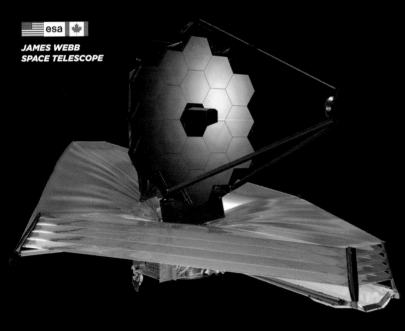

JAMES WEBB SPACE TELESCOPE

CHANDRA'S EYE OPENERS

Deployed in 1999 by the Space Shuttle *Columbia*, the Chandra X-Ray Observatory is a telescope that looks at black holes, starburst galaxies and supernovas. Because it collects X-rays rather than visible light, Chandra can detect things the human eye cannot see. Its observations have included galaxies colliding and a supernova.

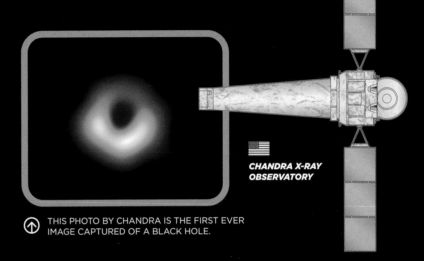

CHANDRA X-RAY OBSERVATORY

⊙ THIS PHOTO BY CHANDRA IS THE FIRST EVER IMAGE CAPTURED OF A BLACK HOLE.

DIFFERENT LIGHT

Earth telescopes work by collecting visible light. But even on a clear night, air currents in the atmosphere can blur a telescope's images. Space telescopes are not hampered by the atmosphere and can detect wavelengths other than visible light. These wavelengths include X-ray, infrared, ultraviolet and microwave. Many telescopes can respond to a combination of different wavelengths to build up a clearer view.

⊙ THIS IMAGE OF PART OF OUR MILKY WAY GALAXY HAS BEEN CREATED BY COMBINING IMAGES IN DIFFERENT WAVELENGTHS FROM THE HUBBLE TELESCOPE, THE SPITZER SPACE TELESCOPE AND THE CHANDRA X-RAY OBSERVATORY.

LOOKING FOR ALIENS

Are aliens out there somewhere in space? There are over 100 billion stars in our galaxy, many with their own systems of planets. Beyond our galaxy, there are billions of galaxies more. Could Earth really be the only world to contain life? But if life is out there, what does it look like – and how do we find it?

SEEKING SETI

The search for alien life is known by the term SETI (Search for Extraterrestrial Intelligence). Various organisations have been founded over the years to scan the skies in the hope of tracking down evidence of alien life. Most of these organisations are financed privately, such as the SETI Institute in California, which was established in 1984. To date, hundreds of millions of dollars have been spent worldwide, but no evidence of extraterrestrial life has been found.

MESSAGING METI

In 2017, an organisation called Messaging Extraterrestrial Intelligence (METI) sent a radio message to two exoplanets orbiting a star called GJ 273, around 12.36 light years from Earth. METI thinks there might be a response in about 25 years – that is, of course, if alien life exists there and can send a message back. However, sending messages into the unknown has provoked some hostility. After all, Earth is a planet rich in resources that could simply be taken from us by a superior species. Others argue that if aliens did pick up a message from Earth, they probably wouldn't be able to understand it anyway.

LOOKING FOR ALIEN LIFE HAS BEEN LIKENED TO DIPPING A CUP IN THE OCEAN. THE CHANCE OF CATCHING A FISH IS SMALL, BUT THAT DOESN'T MEAN THE OCEAN ISN'T FULL OF FISH.

SCIENTISTS INCLUDING THE LATE STEPHEN HAWKING HAVE SAID ATTRACTING ADVANCED ALIEN CIVILISATIONS TO EARTH COULD HAVE TERRIBLE CONSEQUENCES.

THE TESS TELESCOPE

Most astronomers believe that alien life will exist on an exoplanet that, like Earth, orbits its sun in the 'goldilocks' distance range, which allows for liquid water. The Transiting Exoplanet Survey Satellite (TESS) may help find such a planet. TESS is a space telescope in orbit around Earth that aims to find new exoplanets with rocky surfaces like ours. Further observations from ground-based telescopes, as well as space-based ones such as the James Webb Space Telescope (see p.97), will help classify planets as rock worlds or gas giants.

⊕ TO FIND EXOPLANETS TESS WILL SURVEY THE ENTIRE SKY.

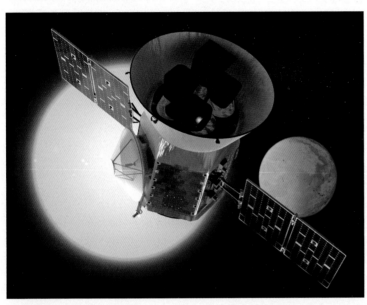

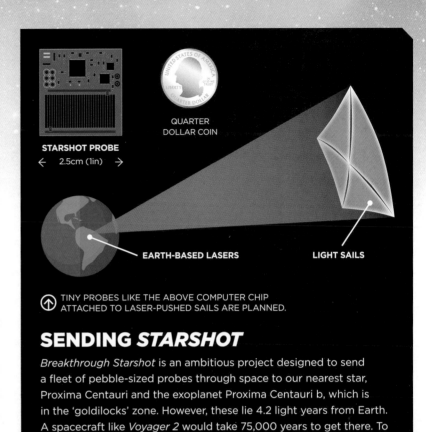

STARSHOT PROBE
← 2.5cm (1in) →

QUARTER DOLLAR COIN

EARTH-BASED LASERS

LIGHT SAILS

⊕ TINY PROBES LIKE THE ABOVE COMPUTER CHIP ATTACHED TO LASER-PUSHED SAILS ARE PLANNED.

SENDING *STARSHOT*

Breakthrough Starshot is an ambitious project designed to send a fleet of pebble-sized probes through space to our nearest star, Proxima Centauri and the exoplanet Proxima Centauri b, which is in the 'goldilocks' zone. However, these lie 4.2 light years from Earth. A spacecraft like *Voyager 2* would take 75,000 years to get there. To speed the journey up, *Breakthrough Starshot* plans to fit its satellites with lightweight sails and beam them across space with a high-powered laser-beam. This would allow the satellites to arrive at Proxima Centauri b in 20 years. Then their search for life could begin.

STAR SHADING THE SUN

To find an exoplanet that might contain life, a space telescope looks at the light coming from it. This light may reveal telltale biosignatures: wavelengths that contain gases associated with life. Other infrared light may show technosignatures, such as polluting gases that rise above cities. Light from any planet is swamped by the brightness of its parent star, so a piece of equipment called Starshade has been devised. This is a spaceship with a large petal-shaped fan designed to fly in front of a space telescope and filter out starlight, so the light from its planets can get through.

①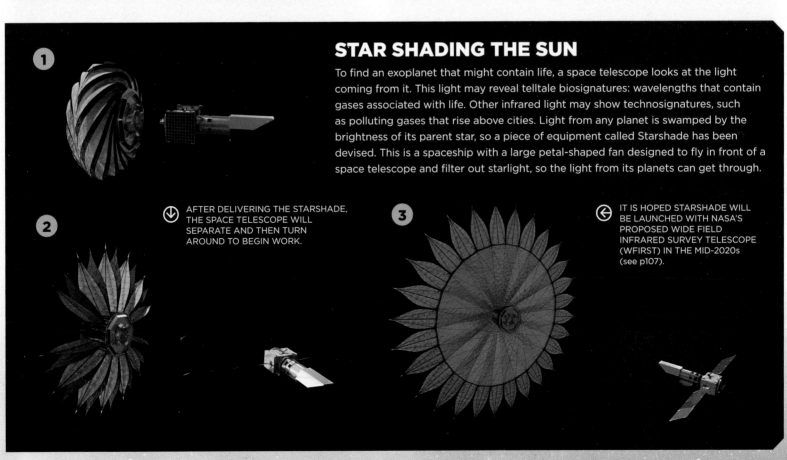

② ⊕ AFTER DELIVERING THE STARSHADE, THE SPACE TELESCOPE WILL SEPARATE AND THEN TURN AROUND TO BEGIN WORK.

③ ⊕ IT IS HOPED STARSHADE WILL BE LAUNCHED WITH NASA'S PROPOSED WIDE FIELD INFRARED SURVEY TELESCOPE (WFIRST) IN THE MID-2020s (see p107).

SPACE EQUIPMENT

Equipment designed for space is among the most technologically advanced in the world. Scientists and engineers are often asked to come up with ingenious solutions for the difficult situations created in space. So, what are the latest developments?

ROBOTS IN SPACE

In August 2019, the first humanoid robot blasted into space for a two-week mission on a *Soyuz* spacecraft. The Russian robot, called Skybot F-850, was not hijacking the craft, but instead starting its mission aboard the *International Space Station* (*ISS*). Equipped with artificial intelligence that allowed it to act independently, Skybot F-850 had robotic hands that could carry out the same tasks as a human. The robot had the *ISS*'s full operational manual downloaded into its databanks and could answer simple questions about the spacecraft if asked. However, Skybot F-850 could only speak Russian.

→ SKYBOT F-850'S HANDS CAN TURN VALVES, UNLOCK DOORS AND WORK AN ELECTRIC DRILL.

NO TICK-TOCK ATOMIC CLOCK

An atomic clock that could change the way spacecraft navigate was launched into Earth's orbit by NASA in 2019. The Deep Space Atomic Clock (DSAC) is more stable than other atomic clocks already in orbit on GPS satellites. Atomic clocks are used to measure distances by timing how long it takes for signals to travel between two points in space. DSAC will lose only one second every 10 million years, which will make the calculation of distances in space much more precise.

WORLD LIFE SCANNER

A scanner that can be taken aboard spacecraft to search for life is under development. It would work by analysing the light reflected from the surfaces of distant planets. The scanner will search for patterns in the light created by molecules that are only made by living creatures. The scanner is being developed at the Netherlands' Leiden University and a first prototype is scheduled to be sent to the *International Space Station* for testing in the early 2020s. If a success, the scanner could then be sent to Saturn's moons Enceladus and Titan, which scientists believe might possibly be inhabited by simple living things.

↑ IN SCIENCE-FICTION MOVIES, SPACESHIPS OFTEN SCAN FOR LIFE BEFORE DESCENDING TO A PLANET'S SURFACE.

MARS MINICOPTER

A small, drone-sized helicopter that attaches to a rover will be sent to Mars as part of NASA's *Mars 2020* mission. This will make the twin-rotor, solar-powered helicopter the first aircraft to be taken to another planet. Here, it will only be used as a test vehicle and will have no scientific equipment aboard. This makes the experiment cost-effective: if the helicopter fails, then no large investment will be lost. If it works, however, the helicopter will likely prove instrumental in investigating hard-to-reach places.

↓ ARTIST'S IMPRESSION OF THE MARS HELICOPTER.

↑ A PROTOTYPE OF NASA'S Z-1, A NEXT GENERATION SPACESUIT.

NEW-GEN SPACESUITS

The Z-1 spacesuit (pictured above) has been developed for use in deep-space missions. Astronauts will have to slip into it through a hatch on the back that can attach to the vehicle they are in. Other recent designs include the Astro spacesuit that was unveiled in late 2019 by the designers of the *Apollo* lunar spacesuits. It uses new fabrics to make it lighter and more mobile. Wearers will have an in-suit digital display system activated by voice commands. The suit can be resized, unlike previous spacesuits that had to be tailored to fit an individual astronaut's body.

SPACE FAILURES

Not everything goes to plan in the fast-paced world of space exploration. In their desperation to win the Space Race, both the United States and Soviet Union cut corners and made mistakes. Ranging from minor accidents to terrible tragedies, these mistakes have continued up until the present day.

APOLLO 1

In its hurry to beat the Soviet Union to the Moon, NASA began cutting corners during the Space Race. This led to the *Apollo 1* disaster on 27 January 1967. It occurred when astronauts Gus Grissom, Ed White and Roger Chaffee were sealed into the Command Module of the *Apollo 1* spacecraft during routine testing. There was a communications breakdown, which had to be fixed while the astronauts were still strapped in. An exposed wire caused a spark, and fire rushed through the module. There was not time to remove the spacecraft's hatch before all three astronauts died.

NASA RECEIVED HEAVY CRITICISM FOR THE *APOLLO 1* DEATHS, BUT ITS SPACE PROGRAMME CONTINUED.

THE BEDSTEAD WAS EQUIPPED WITH AN EJECTOR SEAT CONTAINING THRUSTERS AND A PARACHUTE.

FLYING BEDSTEAD

The Flying Bedstead was the name given to a practice model of the Lunar Module that would land on the Moon. Notoriously difficult to fly, the bedstead gave astronaut Neil Armstrong a brush with death in 1968 when he was practising before his *Apollo 11* mission. While 150m (490ft) above the ground, the bedstead started spinning out of control and Armstrong had to eject before it crashed into the ground in flames. It was a near miss.

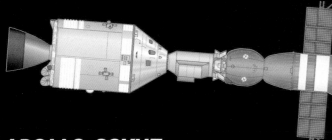

APOLLO-SOYUZ

After the hostility of the Space Race, the United States and Soviet Union agreed to a symbolic handshake in space. This took place on a 1975 docking between an *Apollo* and *Soyuz* craft in orbit. The mission went like clockwork, but during re-entry there was a malfunction aboard *Apollo* that caused unbreathable nitrogen to pour into the craft. Luckily, none of the astronauts died, although they were rushed to hospital upon landing and were ill for several weeks.

TO MAKE THE MEETING EASIER, BOTH SIDES TRIED TO SPEAK THE OTHER'S LANGUAGE.

APOLLO 12

The second manned mission to the Moon was nearly stopped when it was twice struck by lightning. Although the lightning was dangerous enough to damage some of the more delicate systems on board, the mission went ahead as planned and continued without incident until its splashdown in the Atlantic Ocean. Then, a strong wave caused a camera to land on astronaut Alan Bean's head, giving him a 2.5cm (1in) cut.

APOLLO 12 WAS STRUCK BY LIGHTNING TWICE LESS THAN A MINUTE AFTER LAUNCHING ON 14 NOVEMBER 1969.

CHALLENGER AND COLUMBIA

One of the worst events in NASA's history occurred on 28 January 1986. About one minute after taking off, a rubber seal around Space Shuttle *Challenger*'s rocket boosters failed and a fire raced through the craft. The shuttle broke up in mid-air in front of millions of viewers watching live on television. Then, on 1 February 2003, history repeated itself when Space Shuttle *Columbia* disintegrated upon its return to Earth. A hole created at take off caused a wing to fall off during re-entry. Fourteen astronauts died as a result of both shuttle disasters.

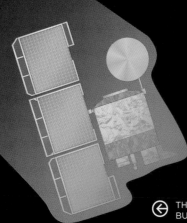

THE MARS CLIMATE ORBITER BURNING UP ON ENTRY

MARS MISTAKES

In the desire to discover more about Mars, there have been some notable mishaps. In 1999, the *Mars Climate Orbiter* mission ended in disaster when the probe burned upon entering Mars' atmosphere. The reason? There was a mix-up between metric and imperial measurements. Then, in 2003 *Beagle 2* successfully landed on Mars but got entangled in its parachute and was unable to complete its mission.

SPACE TOURISM

During the 20th century, only governments had the means to send people into space. Even then the best astronauts and cosmonauts had to train for years to be given the chance to join a space mission. But now money is all you need.

SOYUZ

SPACEX DRAGON CREW

BOEING STARLINER

TOURISTS TO SPACE

American businessman Dennis Tito became the first space tourist in 2001 when he paid a reported USD$20 million to stay aboard the *International Space Station* (*ISS*) for six days. NASA was originally against the idea, but saw the advantages of having people pay to visit the *ISS*. After cancelling its Space Shuttle programme, NASA has had to pay Russia to use its *Soyuz* spacecraft to visit the *ISS*. By accepting space tourists to the *ISS*, the US will raise funds for its own space programme. In 2019, NASA announced it would consider sending two space tourists to the *ISS* every year and studios could even film movies there.

BOEING

Aeroplane manufacturer Boeing is another company preparing for space tourism to the *ISS* by developing its *CST-100 Starliner*. The *Starliner* has a similar shape to the *Apollo* spacecraft, but with a more modern and advanced interior. The craft will carry seven tourists dressed in Boeing's custom-made blue spacesuits. These are lighter than the previous bulky NASA spacesuits and include gloves that can be used with touchpad screens. The gumdrop-shaped *Starliner* capsule will be able to remain in orbit for six months at a time and could be reused up to 10 times.

⬅ THE *STARLINER* CAPSULE WILL BLAST INTO SPACE ON TOP OF AN *ATLAS 5* ROCKET.

SPACEX

In 2019, private American company SpaceX announced that it would work with NASA to send tourists to the *ISS* for around USD$52 million a ticket. The ticket would pay for one to two months in space. The first tourists should be able to visit in the 2020s aboard SpaceX's *Crew Dragon* capsule. SpaceX was the first private company to send supplies to the *ISS* aboard its *Dragon* spacecraft. If the *ISS* trips go well, SpaceX has said that it will then try to send people to the Moon.

⬆ ARTIST'S IMPRESSION OF THE *CREW DRAGON* CAPSULE, WHICH WILL SEAT SEVEN PEOPLE.

⬆ THE *DRAGON* CARGO SHIP DOCKING WITH THE *ISS* IN 2014.

VIRGIN

The Virgin company has been offering tickets aboard its suborbital spaceplane *SpaceShipTwo* for several years, although it's yet to fly its first paying passengers. The programme has been beset with problems, including the death of one of its pilots after a test-flight crash in 2014. In December 2018, *SpaceShipTwo* reached the edge of space for the first time and in February 2019 astronaut instructor Beth Moses became *SpaceShipTwo*'s first test passenger. Over 600 people from 60 countries have spent USD$100,000 each to secure a seat on a *SpaceShipTwo* flight, but no scheduled date has been announced for its first commercial departure.

⊘ SPACESHIPTWO DOESN'T TAKE OFF FROM THE GROUND. IT'S CARRIED INTO THE UPPER ATMOSPHERE ATTACHED TO ANOTHER PLANE (SHOWN HERE) FROM WHERE IT LAUNCHES INTO SPACE.

⊕ THE REUSABLE *SPACESHIPTWO* IS DESIGNED TO CARRY SIX PASSENGERS FOR A 180-MINUTE SUBORBITAL FLIGHT, WHICH WILL INCLUDE A FEW MINUTES IN SPACE.

BLUE ORIGIN

Blue Origin is another private company offering suborbital flights – aboard its *New Shepard* vehicle. Named after Alan Shepard, the first US astronaut in space, the *New Shepard* is a reusable rocket that can take off and land in a vertical position. Passengers will therefore be launched straight up to an altitude of around 100km (62 miles) to experience a few moments of weightlessness before descending to the surface again. The whole flight takes around 10 minutes and the cost of a ticket is reported to be between USD$100,000 and USD$300,000.

⊖ THE *NEW SHEPARD* ORBITAL LAUNCH VEHICLE TAKING OFF.

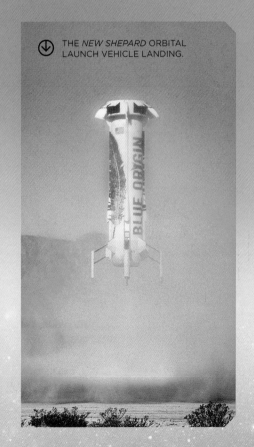

⊘ THE *NEW SHEPARD* ORBITAL LAUNCH VEHICLE LANDING.

FUTURE OF SPACE EXPLORATION

Many remarkable breakthroughs have been made in the short story of space exploration. But compared to the vastness of space, we have not ventured far. So, what is next? Will we colonise planets within our own Solar System or emigrate beyond into the vast, black unknown? What is the future for humanity in space?

LUNAR BASE

The idea of building a permanently manned base on the Moon has been in discussion for several years. Plans for a base have even been drawn up by the European Space Agency. A base on the Moon would offer a chance for people to adapt to living in space, and also act as a springboard for further missions to Mars. With the rise of private companies building their own spacecraft, space exploration is no longer the domain of governments alone. A privately owned lunar base constructed to mine the Moon's resources, such as water ice, minerals and metals, is a real possibility for the near future.

ⓘ NASA HOPES TO HAVE A PERMANENT MANNED PRESENCE ON THE MOON BY 2028.

LIFE ON MARS

Mars was once a planet somewhat like Earth. There is no oxygen there to breathe now, but learning to adapt to this is considered a necessary first step in the human colonisation of new worlds. A Mars base would probably start as an outpost made of self-contained modules, like the *International Space Station*. As more colonists arrived, more modules would be added. The first ones could consist of a laboratory, a science module, a habitat module and a module to grow vegetables.

ⓘ SOME PRIVATE COMPANIES HAVE SUGGESTED A SIMPLE MARS BASE COULD BE CONSTRUCTED AS EARLY AS 2028.

GIANT TELESCOPES

New space telescopes are being built to scan distant space for exoplanets. These telescopes include the Wide Field Infrared Survey Telescope (WFIRST). Planned to be launched in the mid-2020s, WFIRST has a five-year mission. It is hoped this will lead to the discovery of around 2600 new exoplanets.

HUBBLE TELESCOPE FIELD OF VIEW

WFIRST TELESCOPE FIELD OF VIEW

⬆ THE WFIRST SHOULD HAVE A MUCH WIDER FIELD OF VIEW THAN HUBBLE.

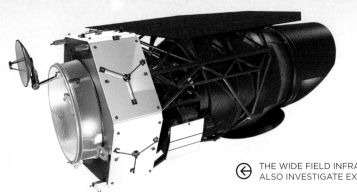

⬅ THE WIDE FIELD INFRARED SURVEY TELESCOPE WILL ALSO INVESTIGATE EXPLODING STARS, CALLED SUPERNOVAS.

NEW SPACE STATIONS

In 2019, NASA announced it would start accepting regular tourists to the *International Space Station* from 2020. A hotel-type module to be attached to the *ISS* has been discussed. The *ISS* is due to finish its life and splash down into the Pacific Ocean in 2030. By then several new space stations are expected to be in orbit around Earth. A mix of government-owned and private enterprises, these new space stations are expected to serve a range of functions, from space tourism to conducting experiments in microgravity. Both are thought necessary if a permanent human presence in space is going to be maintained.

⬅ THE HUMAN OCCUPATION OF THE EARTH'S LOW ORBIT COULD INCREASINGLY BECOME THE DOMAIN OF PRIVATE COMPANIES IN THE NEAR FUTURE.

DRAGONFLY

Saturn's moon Titan contains liquid methane and ethane, and has a nitrogen atmosphere. Scientists believe it could provide a new world for humans to colonise. *Dragonfly* is a nuclear-powered spacecraft that is scheduled to launch in 2026. The craft will consist of a drone and a lander rolled into one. Once it has reached Titan in 2034, *Dragonfly* will begin a series of short 8km (5 mile) flights to explore a dark region called Shangri-La. By the time its five-year mission is complete, it is hoped *Dragonfly* will have discovered signs of microscopic life – either present or potential.

⬅ *DRAGONFLY* WILL ANALYSE TITAN'S SURFACE IN EACH PLACE IT LANDS.

Some of the words in this book are out of this world and others are scientific or technical terms used by people who work in space exploration. If you're not sure what something means, check out the list below...

ARMSTRONG LIMIT

Altitude of about 18km (11 miles) above Earth where the air pressure is so low that liquids on the body's surface start to boil. This includes the liquid on the lungs, so it becomes impossible to breathe without a pressure suit.

ASTEROIDS

Small worlds of rock and metal that orbit the Sun.

BIOSIGNATURE

Something measurable, such as a pattern of light revealing liquid water, which shows that life might be present on another world.

BLACK HOLE

Object in which a lot of matter is crushed into a tiny space, so that the gravity becomes so powerful that even light cannot escape. Huge stars sometimes become black holes when they run out of fuel.

COMET

A large lump of dust and ice which grows one or more tails of ice and dust when it approaches the Sun.

COMMAND AND SERVICE MODULE

The part of an *Apollo* spacecraft in which the astronauts travelled to the Moon's orbit and back.

CONSTELLATION

Pattern of bright stars in the night sky, often named after a mythological character.

COSMONAUT

Russian or Soviet astronaut.

COSMOS (UNIVERSE)

Everything that exists.

CRATER

A bowl-shaped depression found on many rocky planets, moons and asteroids. Most were made billions of years ago by the impact of huge rocks which fell from space.

DWARF PLANET

A world which is smaller than a planet but large enough to be round. Five have been found in our Solar System so far.

ELLIPSE

An oval. All orbits are elliptical.

ESCAPE VELOCITY

The speed a spacecraft must reach in order to completely escape from the gravity of the body it is launched from.

EXOPLANET

Planet going round a star other than the Sun.

EXOSPHERE

In large planets like Earth, the exosphere is the outer part of the atmosphere, where the air is so thin it is almost the same as empty space. The very thin atmospheres of small worlds are also called exospheres.

EXTRAVEHICULAR ACTIVITY (EVA)

Anything an astronaut does in space when (s)he is outside a spacecraft.

FREE FALL

A spacecraft or astronaut is in free fall when their engines are not firing, whether they are flying through space, or orbiting the Earth or another world. See MICROGRAVITY.

G-FORCE (GRAVITATIONAL FORCE)

The force (pull) on an object or person when on the surface of a planet (or other world) or when being accelerated (speeded up).

GRAVITATIONAL SLINGSHOT

A technique in which the gravity of a world is used to change the speed and direction of a spacecraft which passes close by.

ION

An atom or molecule with an electric charge.

KINETIC ENERGY

The energy an object has when it moves.

LANDER

Type of unmanned spacecraft that lands on the surface of a planet or other world.

METEOR OR SHOOTING STAR

Glowing track in the atmosphere caused by the burning-up of a meteoroid when it falls from space.

METEORITE

The remains of a meteoroid which has fallen from space and landed on Earth.

METEOROID

Small piece of rock or metal that travels through space.

MICROGRAVITY

When a spacecraft is in free fall, it and the people and things inside are almost weightless. But all the objects make their own tiny gravity-pulls, and slight changes of speed cause slight g-forces too. This near-weightlessness is called microgravity.

MILKY WAY
The name of the galaxy that includes our Sun and Solar System. It looks like a long smear of milk in the night sky.

MODULE
A detachable part of a spacecraft.

NEAR EARTH OBJECT (NEO)
Any natural object which passes close to Earth. Most are asteroids, and some are comets.

ORBIT
The path of one object around another in space.

ORBITER
Unmanned probe sent to orbit another world.

ORGANIC MATERIAL
Any complex chemical containing carbon. Living things are made of organic chemicals.

PAYLOAD
Whatever a spacecraft carries which it does not use to fly, such as supplies and scientific equipment.

PLANET
A large round world in orbit round a star.

PROBE
A spacecraft with no crew on board, sent to study other worlds.

PROPELLANT
Rocket fuel, together with the oxidiser it needs to burn.

RADIATION BELTS
Region surrounding a planet in which electrons and other charged particles are trapped by the planet's magnetic field.

ROVER
A vehicle, either manned or robotic, used to explore the surface of a planet or moon.

SATELLITE
A natural satellite is a moon; an artificial satellite is a machine placed in orbit by a spacecraft.

SEISMIC
Relating to vibrations that affect the surface of the Earth or other world, usually caused by earthquakes.

SOLAR FLARE
An eruption of radiation from a small area on the surface of the Sun.

SOLAR SYSTEM
The Sun and all the planets, moons, comets and other things which go around it.

SOLAR WIND
Electrically charged particles that travel from the Sun across the Solar System.

SPACE JUNK
Rubbish in orbit round the Earth, left behind from space missions. It includes dead satellites, discarded rocket STAGES, paint fragments and dust particles.

SPEED OF LIGHT
Speed at which light moves. Nothing can travel faster.

STAGE
A detachable part of a rocket that contains its own engine and PROPELLANT.

SUBORBITAL
Relating to a spaceflight that reaches space but does not achieve the velocity needed to go into Earth's orbit.

TERMINATION SHOCK
The 'bubble' surrounding the Solar System where the SOLAR WIND suddenly slows down. Some astronomers think of this as the outer edge of the Solar System.

TRANSIT
The passing of a planet across the face of the Sun, as seen from another planet. From Earth, we can see transits of Venus and Mercury.

VAPORISE
To change a solid or liquid substance into a gas.

VELOCITY
Speed of an object moving in a certain direction.

THE COMPLETE GUIDE TO SPACE EXPLORATION

Project managed by: Dynamo Limited
Author: Ben Hubbard
Commissioning editor: Joe Fullman
Editor: Dynamo Limited
Art director: Andy Mansfield
Design and illustration: Dynamo Limited
Technical illustration: Richard Kruse
Publishing Director: Piers Pickard
Publisher: Hanna Otero
Print Production: Lisa Taylor

Published in September 2020 by Lonely Planet Global Limited

ISBN: 978 1 83869 086 1

www.lonelyplanetkids.com
© Lonely Planet 2020

10 9 8 7 6 5 4 3 2 1

Printed in Malaysia

STAY IN TOUCH
lonelyplanet.com/contact

LONELY PLANET OFFICES

AUSTRALIA
The Malt Store, Level 3, 551 Swanston St, Carlton, Victoria 3053
T: 03 8379 8000

IRELAND
Digital Depot, Roe Lane (off Thomas St), Digital Hub, Dublin 8, D08 TCV4

UNITED KINGDOM
240 Blackfriars Rd, London SE1 8NW
T: 020 3771 5100

USA
Suite 208, 155 Filbert Street, Oakland, CA 94607
T: 510 250 6400

Paper in this book is certified against the Forest Stewardship Council™ standards. FSC™ promotes environmentally responsible, socially beneficial and economically viable management of the world's forests.

PICTURE CREDITS

The publisher would like to thank the following for their kind permission to reproduce their photographs:

(Key: a-above; b-below/bottom; c-centre; f-far; l-left; r-right; t-top)

Page 2/3 (b) NASA /J PL-Caltech ; **Page 4** (l) NASA, (r) NASA / JPL-Caltech / MSSS ; **Page 5** (cl) NASA, ESA, and S. Beckwith (STScI) and the HUDF Team, (cr) ESA / P. Carril ; **Page 6** (t) NASA, (cr) Getty Images / Fine Art Images / Heritage Images (b) NASA ; **Page 7** (cr) NASA, (bl) NASA, (br) NASA / JPL ; **Page 8** (b) Shutterstock / Erkki Makkonen (b) Shutterstock / Ivan Kurmyshov (r) Shutterstock / ployy ; **Page 9** (tl) Alamy / Science History Images, (tr) Alamy / Peter Horree, (bl) Alamy / Science History Images ; **Page 10** (l) Alamy / The Picture Art Collection, (b) Alamy / Stocktrek Images, Inc., (r) Alamy / World History Archive, (r) Shutterstock / Lia Koltyrina ; **Page 11** (l) National Geographic Image Collection / Alamy Stock Photo, (br) Shutterstock /Linda Moon ; **Page 12** (fl) Alamy / Archive World, (bl) Alamy / Artokoloro Quint Lox Limited, (r) Alamy / ITAR-TASS News Agency ; **Page 13** (l) NASA, (r) Chronicle / Alamy Stock Photo ; **Page 14** (l) Alamy / Photo 12, (b) Alamy / RGB Ventures / SuperStock, (r) Getty Images / US Army / The LIFE Picture Collection ; **Page 15** (l) Alamy / SPUTNIK (t) Alamy / Shawshots ; **Page 16** (l) NASA / U.S. Navy, (tr) NASA ; **Page 17** (t) NASA / JPL ; **Page 18** (l) NASA , (b) ESA / P. Carril ; **Page 19** (tr) NASA ; **Page 20** (l) Alamy / Heritage Image Partnership Ltd, (t) Getty Images / Keystone / Stringer (tr) Getty Images / Hulton-Deutsch Collection / CORBIS (r) NASA / Marshall Space Flight Center ; **Page 21** (l) NASA, (tr) NASA, (cr) Getty Images / Science Photo Library / STEVE GSCHMEISSNER ; **Page 22** (l) Getty Images / Heritage Images ; **Page 24** (l) NASA, (r) Getty Images / Bettmann ; **Page 25** (l) NASA, (r) Getty Images / Keystone / Staff, (b) NASA ; **Page 26** (l) Shutterstock / DinhoR10 (tr) NASA ; **Page 27** (tl) AFP via Getty Images, (r) NASA ; **Page 28/29** (all images) NASA ; **Page 30** (t) NASA ; **Page 31** (tr) Alamy / Dan Leeth ; **Page 32** (t) Shutterstock / Kal Pycco ; **Page 33** (t) NASA, (b) NASA ; **Page 34 / 35** (all) NASA ; **Page 38** (l) NASA, (r) NASA ; **Page 39** (br) NASA ; **Page 40** (tl) NASA, (bl) Shutterstock / Raymond Cassel, (cb) NASA / Goddard / Arizona State University ; **Page 41** (tl) CNSA/CLEP/CAS (r) ESA - P. Carril, (br) NASA ; **Page 42** (tr) Shutterstock / amskad ; **Page 44** (l) NASA, (c) NASA / Alex Gerst ; **Page 45** (bl) NASA, (tr) NASA, (br) Getty Images / Joe Raedle ; **Page 46/47** (c) NASA / Roscosmos ; **Page 50** (l) NASA / Johns Hopkins University Applied Physics Laboratory / Carnegie Institution of Washington, (c) NASA / Johns Hopkins University Applied Physics Laboratory / Carnegie Institution of Washington. (br) NASA / SDO / HMI / AIA ; **Page 51** (r) ESA/ATG medialab ; **Page 52** (bl) NASA/Johns Hopkins University Applied Physics Laboratory / Carnegie Institution of Washington, (br) NASA's Goddard Space Flight Center / SDO ; **Page 53** NASA / Johns Hopkins University Applied Physics Laboratory / Carnegie Institution of Washington ; **Page 54** (l) NASA, (r) NASA/JPL, (c) NASA / JPL ; **Page 55** (bl) Sovfoto / Universal Images Group via Getty Images, (br) NASA / JPL ; **Page 56** (l) NASA, (r) ESA ; **Page 58** (l) ASA / JPL-Caltech, (c) NASA / JPL /USGS, (b) NASA / GSFC ; **Page 59** (bl) NASA / JPL-Caltech, (br) NASA / JPL / USGS ; **Page 61** (c) NASA / JPL-Caltech / MSSS ; **Page 62** (bl) NASA / JPL-Caltech / ESA / DLR / FU Berlin / MSSS ; **Page 63** (c) NASA / JPL/Cornell, (tr) NASA / JPL-Caltech, (tr) NASA / JPL-Caltech ; **Page 64** (l) NASA / JPL, (r) NASA / JPL-Caltech/Univ. of Arizona ; **Page 66** (c) NASA / JPL / Björn Jónsson (b) NASA / JPL / Cornell University ; **Page 67** (br) NASA / ESA / J. Nichols (University of Leicester) ; **Page 68** (l) NASA ; **Page 69** (t) H. Hammel / MIT / NASA, (tl) NASA / JPL, (tr) NASA / JPL, (cl) NASA / JPL, (c) NASA / JPL / Ted Stryk, (cr) NASA/JPL/University of Arizona, (bl) NASA / JPL / DLR, (br) NASA / JPL / DLR ; **Page 70** (cl) NASA / JPL-Caltech / SETI Institute (br) NASA /J PL ; **Page 71** (br) NASA / JPL-Caltech / SwRI / MSSS / Kevin M. Gill ; **Page 72** (cl) NASA Ames, (c) NASA / JPL / Space Science Institute, (br) NASA / JPL-Caltech / Space Science Institute ; **Page 73** (cr) NASA / JPL-Caltech / Space Science Institute, (b) NASA / JPL-Caltech / SSI ; **Page 74** (cr) ESA / NASA / JPL / University of Arizona ; **Page 75** (tl) NASA / JPL-Caltech / ASI / Cornell, (tc) NASA / JPL-Caltech / Space Science Institute, (tr) NASA / JPL-Caltech / Space Science Institute, (bl) NASA/JPL-Caltech/ Space Science Institute, (br) Getty Images / MARK GARLICK / SCIENCE PHOTO LIBRARY ; **Page 76** (cl) NASA / JPL-Caltech / SSI / Kevin M. Gill, (br) NASA / JPL-Caltech ; **Page 77** (br) NASA / JPL-Caltech / Space Science Institute ; **Page 78** (cl) NASA / JPL, (tr) NASA / JPL-Caltech, (bl) Lawrence Sromovsky, University of Wisconsin-Madison / W.W. Keck Observatory ; **Page 79** (br) NASA / JPL-Caltech ; **Page 80** (l) Alamy / Science Photo Library, (br) Getty Images / Stocktrek Images ; **Page 82** (c) NASA / Johns Hopkins University Applied Physics Laboratory / Southwest Research Institute, (cl) NASA / Johns Hopkins University Applied Physics Laboratory / Southwest Research Institute ; **Page 83** (tr) NASA / Johns Hopkins University Applied Physics Laboratory / Southwest Research Institute, (c) NASA / Johns Hopkins Applied Physics Laboratory / Southwest Research Institute, National Optical Astronomy Observatory ; **Page 84** (c) NASA / JPL-Caltech Photojournal ; **Page 85** (c) NASA / JPL ; **Page 86** (bl) PARKER SOLAR PROBE/NASA AND NAVAL RESEARCH LABORATORY, (c) NASA / Goddard / SDO ; **Page 87** (tc) NASA/Goddard Space Flight Center, (cr) NASA ; **Page 88** (tl) NASA / JPL (tr) NASA / JPL (b) NASA / JPL / JHUAPL (bl) Shutterstock / AuntSpray ; **Page 89** (tl) NASA / JPL-Caltech / UCLA / MPS / DLR / IDA, (tr) NASA / JPL-Caltech / UCLA / MPS / DLR / IDA / Justin Cowart, (bc) Alamy Stock Photo / Newscom ; **Page 90** (l) Getty Images / DEA / G. DAGLI ORTI, (bl) ESA / MPAe Lindau, (cr) ESA / Rosetta / MPS for OSIRIS Team MPS / UPD / LAM / IAA / SSO / INTA / UPM / DASP /I DA ; **Page 91** (cl) ESA / ATG medialab, (tr) NASA / JPL-Caltech / UMD, (br) NASA / JPL ; **Page 92** (l) ESA, (br) ESO / E. Slawik ; **Page 93** (bl) Alamy / Science History Images ; **Page 94** (fl) NASA, (c) Getty Images / HENNING DALHOFF, (r) NASA / JPL-Caltech / ESO / R. Hurt ; **Page 95** (l) SCIENCE PHOTO LIBRARY / MIKKEL JUUL JENSEN, (r) NASA, ESA, G. Illingworth and D. Magee (University of California, Santa Cruz), K. Whitaker (University of Connecticut), R. Bouwens (Leiden University), P. Oesch (University of Geneva) and the Hubble Legacy Field team ; **Page 96** (l) NASA, (r) NASA / Ames / JPL-Caltech ; **Page 97** (l) NASA, (r) Event Horizon Telescope collaboration et al., (b) NASA / JPL-Caltech / ESA / CXC / STScI ; **Page 98** (l) Shutterstpock / zhengzaishuru, (r) Shutterstpock / Greg Mathieso ; **Page 99** (l) NASA's Goddard Space Flight Center, (b) NASA / JPL-Caltech ; **Page 100** (l) NASA, (r) Getty images / Stanislav Krasilnikov / Contributor ; **Page 101** (t) Getty images / MATJAZ SLANIC, (b) NASA / JPL-Caltech, (r) NASA ; **Page 102** (l) NASA, (t) NASA, (br) Shutterstock / Everett Historical ; **Page 104** (c) NASA, (bl) NASA, (br) NASA / SpaceX, (c) NASA/Joel Kowsky ; **Page 105** (l) Getty Images / GENE BLEVINS, (r) MARK RALSTON/AFP via Getty Images, (bl) (br) Alamy Stock Photo / Blue Horizon ; **Page 106** (bl) NASA, (c) Getty Images / luissmmolina, (tr) NASA / JPL / USGS, (l) NASA / GSFC / Arizona State University ; **Page 107** (l) NASA, (tr) NASA, ESA, PHAT Team, (bl) NASA, (cr) Shutterstock / Robusot, (br) NASA / JPL-Caltech / Space Science Institute

Technical illustrations by Richard Kruse at HistoricSpacecraft.com: **Page 5** (bl), **Page 15** (br), **Page 22** (c), **Page 23** (bl), **Page 34** (tr), **Page 37** (b), (r), **Page 42** (b) x 14, **Page 47** (r) x 4, **Page 49** (t) x 5, 51 (tl) x2, **Page 55** (tl) x 5, **Page 59** (tl) x4, (cr) x 4, **Page 60** (tl), **Page 67** (tl) x 4, (bl), **Page 69** (bl), (tr) x 2, **Page 73** (tl) x 3, **Page 74** (tr), **Page 79** (tl) x 2, **Page P83** (tl), **Page 85** (tl), **Page 87** (tl) x 2, **Page 88** (c), (bc), **Page 89** (tl), (cl), **Page 90** (bl), (t), **Page 91** (tr), (cr), **Page 98** (bl), (mr), **Page 99** (mr), **Page 103** (tl), **Page 104** (tr),

All other illustrations Dynamo Limited. Background images/icons: Getty Images, Dreamstime and Dynamo Limited